HR REMOTELY

How To Create A Remote Workforce

Michael Kennedy

Capitol Management LLC

CAPITOL
MANAGEMENT LLC

ISBN-13 979-8-218-11895-2
ISBN-13 979-8-218-11894-5

Printed in the United States of America

CONTENTS

FOREWORD

As a human resources professional who has managed remote teams, I know firsthand the challenges that come with keeping a virtual workforce motivated and engaged. That's why I'm thrilled to be introducing my new book, HR Remotely: How to Motivate a Remote Workforce.

In this book, I draw on my experience managing remote teams as an Human Resources Director and consulting with companies on HR-related issues to provide practical strategies for motivating remote workers. From creating a positive work culture to providing effective communication and feedback, I offer actionable solutions to help employers build a successful remote work environment.

One of the things I am most proud of in this book is my ability to provide real-world examples and case studies that illustrate my points. By showcasing successful strategies and highlighting common pitfalls to avoid, I hope to provide readers with the tools they need to build a motivated and productive remote workforce.

Whether you are a seasoned HR professional or new to managing remote teams, I believe that HR Remotely has something valuable to offer. By providing a comprehensive guide to remote workforce motivation, this book can help you create a more engaged and productive virtual team, regardless of your industry or company size.

At Capitol Management LLC, we specialize in providing customized solutions to help you build and lead a high-performing remote team. Our team of experts has years of experience working with businesses across a range of industries, and we have a proven track record of success in helping our clients achieve their goals.

Whether you're struggling to engage and motivate your remote team, or you're looking for ways to improve communication and collaboration, we can help. With our comprehensive consulting services, we'll work with you to develop a tailored approach that meets your specific needs and delivers results.

I hope that the insights and strategies shared in this book will be valuable to you as you strive to motivate your remote team. And if you're looking for additional support and guidance, I invite you to visit our website at https://capitolmanager.com and explore the consulting services that we offer.

I invite you to join me on this journey and discover the many benefits of a motivated remote workforce. Thank you for choosing HR Remotely as your guide to remote workforce motivation, and I look forward to the opportunity to work with you and help your business thrive.

◆◆◆

INTRODUCTION

Motivating Remote Workers in the Digital Age

The digital age has brought about significant changes in the way we work. With the rise of remote work and distributed teams, it is now possible to work from anywhere in the world, with just a laptop and an internet connection. While this shift towards remote work has many advantages, it also presents unique challenges, especially when it comes to motivating and engaging remote workers.

Motivating remote workers is a critical factor for the success of any remote team. Without the right motivation, remote workers may struggle to stay productive, focused, and engaged in their work, which can ultimately impact the success of the team and the organization.

In this book, we will explore practical strategies for motivating remote workers and fostering a positive work culture in the digital age. We will begin by discussing the challenges of remote work and the importance of motivation for remote workers, before moving on to specific strategies for motivating remote workers, including creating a positive work culture, providing effective communication and feedback, setting clear expectations and goals, and promoting work-life balance.

Chapter 1:Overview of Remote Work and Its Challenges

In this chapter, we will provide an overview of remote work and its challenges. We will explore the benefits and drawbacks of remote work, the rise of remote work in the digital age, and the unique challenges that remote work presents for both employees and employers. We will also discuss the importance of motivation for remote workers and how it impacts job satisfaction, engagement, and productivity.

Chapter 2: Understanding Motivation

Here we explore the various theories of motivation and how motivation works.. This chapter discusses Maslow's Hierarchy of Needs, Herzberg's Two-Factor Theory, and Self-Determination Theory. It explains intrinsic and extrinsic motivation, rewards, recognition, and goal-setting. The chapter emphasizes the challenges remote workers face and the need for a motivating work environment. It highlights the importance of communication, feedback, and building relationships to keep remote workers motivated.

Chapter 3: Creating a Motivating Remote Work Culture

This chapter provides practical strategies to build a remote work culture that promotes motivation and engagement. The chapter covers identifying company values and goals, establishing communication channels, building team culture, encouraging collaboration, and creating an inclusive work environment. It emphasizes the need for clear communication, team-building activities, promoting diversity, and equity.

Chapter 4: Setting Clear Expectations and Goals for Remote Workers

Setting clear expectations and goals is critical for motivating remote workers and ensuring that they are aligned with the organization's objectives. In this chapter, we will explore strategies for setting clear expectations and goals, including establishing performance metrics, providing regular performance reviews, and creating a culture of accountability.

Chapter 5: Promoting Work-Life Balance for Remote Workers

Promoting work-life balance is essential for maintaining the well-being of remote workers and preventing burnout. In this chapter, we will discuss strategies for promoting work-life balance, including establishing boundaries between work and personal life, providing flexible work arrangements, and promoting self-care.

Chapter 6: Empowering Remote Workers

Chapter 6 of this book is dedicated to the topic of empowering remote workers. With the growing trend of remote work, it has become more important than ever for companies to understand how to support and empower their remote employees. This chapter explores various strategies that organizations can use to empower their remote workers, including trusting employees to take ownership of their work, providing autonomy and flexibility, encouraging innovation and creativity, and offering opportunities for growth and development. By implementing these strategies, companies can build a strong remote work culture that fosters trust, collaboration, and productivity.

Chapter 7: Communication Strategies for Remote Teams

With the physical distance between team members in a remote work environment, effective communication becomes critical for successful collaboration and teamwork. This chapter will explore various communication strategies that companies can use to build trust among remote team members, including selecting the right communication tools, establishing regular check-ins and meetings, and promoting open and transparent communication. By implementing these strategies, companies can enhance collaboration, productivity, and job satisfaction among their remote teams.

Chapter 8: Motivating Through Recognition and Rewards

Motivating remote workers can be challenging, but providing meaningful recognition and rewards can help keep remote employees engaged and motivated. In this chapter, we will explore various strategies for recognizing and rewarding remote workers, such as developing a recognition and rewards program, creating a culture of appreciation, and choosing the right incentives for remote employees. By implementing these strategies, companies can help increase employee satisfaction, retention, and productivity among their remote workforce.

Chapter 9: Overcoming Challenges and Barriers

Although remote work offers numerous benefits, it also presents unique challenges that companies need to address. In this chapter, we will discuss various challenges of remote work, including communication barriers, time zone differences, and supporting remote workers in different cultures. We will explore different strategies that companies can use to overcome these challenges and create a successful remote work environment. By implementing these strategies, companies can ensure that their remote teams are productive, engaged, and successful despite the challenges that remote work may present.

Chapter 10: Tools and Technologies to Support Remote Work Motivation

Technology plays a critical role in enabling remote work, and it is important for companies to select the right tools to support their remote teams. In this chapter, we will discuss various tools and technologies that can enhance remote work productivity and motivation. We will also explore how to maximize the benefits of technology while addressing its downsides, such as the potential for isolation and overreliance on technology. By implementing the right tools and technologies, companies can create a successful remote work environment that enables their teams to work efficiently and effectively, while staying motivated and engaged.

Chapter 11: Best Practices for Remote Work Motivation

In this chapter, we will discuss tips for motivating remote workers, best practices for remote work success, and how to address common pitfalls that can arise when working remotely. We will also explore how to create a sustainable remote work culture that promotes motivation, engagement, and productivity. By implementing these best practices, companies can ensure that their remote teams are successful and that their remote work culture is sustainable in the long term.

Chapter 12: Conclusion

Chapter 12 is the conclusion of the book, summarizing key points on motivating remote workers, overcoming challenges, and selecting the right tools and technologies. It emphasizes the importance of motivation for remote work success and provides recommendations for creating a sustainable remote work culture. The chapter highlights the benefits of remote work and offers practical recommendations such as communication, growth opportunities, and trust.

◆◆◆

CHAPTER 1

Overview of Remote Work and Its Challenges

Remote work is a work arrangement that allows employees to work from outside of a traditional office environment, often from their homes or a location of their choosing. The rise of remote work has been driven by several factors, including advances in technology, changing attitudes towards work-life balance, and the need for cost savings by employers.

The COVID-19 pandemic has also accelerated the trend towards remote work, with many companies transitioning their employees to remote work arrangements to maintain business continuity and reduce the risk of spreading the virus. As a result, remote work has become a more mainstream way of working, with many employees and employers embracing the benefits of working remotely.

According to a survey conducted by Global Workplace Analytics, remote work has increased by 159% over the last decade, with approximately 4.7 million employees working remotely in the US alone in 2021.[1]A 2020 study by Upwork found that 36.2 million Americans will be working remotely by 2025, an 87% increase from pre-pandemic levels.[2]While remote work offers many benefits, such as increased flexibility and work-life balance, it also presents unique challenges for both employees and employers.

Benefits of Remote Work

1. Increased Flexibility

Remote work has emerged as a popular employment option for millions of people around the world. The freedom and flexibility that comes with working remotely is one of the major reasons why this work style has become increasingly popular. The ability to work from anywhere, at any time, and on any device, provides remote workers with a level of flexibility that traditional office jobs cannot offer. In this chapter, we will explore the many benefits of increased flexibility in remote work.

One of the key benefits of remote work is that it allows employees to create a work schedule that fits their lifestyle. Remote work provides individuals with the ability to structure their workday in a way that suits their personal needs and preferences. For instance, remote workers may choose to start their workday earlier than the traditional 9-to-5 office hours to allow for more time in the afternoon for personal activities. This flexibility is particularly beneficial for individuals with families, as they can spend more time with their children, attend school events, or care for a loved one.

The flexibility of remote work can also benefit employees who have to commute long distances to work. Long commutes can be draining and can take a toll on an individual's physical and mental health. Remote work eliminates the need for a daily commute, reducing stress, saving time and money, and improving overall well-being.

Furthermore, the flexibility of remote work can benefit employers as well. Companies that offer remote work options often see a decrease in employee absenteeism and an increase in productivity. By allowing employees to structure their workday around their personal needs, remote work can boost employee morale and job satisfaction. When employees feel valued and supported, they are more likely to be engaged and productive on the job.

Remote work is also beneficial for companies that operate across different time zones or have clients or customers in different parts of the world. Remote workers can adjust their schedules to ensure that they are available during critical times or to work with colleagues in different time zones. This allows for greater collaboration and teamwork, improving the quality of work and customer satisfaction.

Another benefit of increased flexibility in remote work is the ability to work from anywhere. This flexibility can be particularly beneficial for individuals who have to travel frequently for work or have family obligations that require them to be in different locations. Remote work allows employees to work from anywhere with an internet connection, making it possible to work from home, a coffee shop, or even while traveling.

Finally, remote work can also provide individuals with the opportunity to pursue their interests and passions outside of work. With a more flexible work schedule, remote workers can devote time to hobbies, volunteer work, or other personal interests. This can lead to a more fulfilling and balanced life, which in turn can lead to greater overall happiness and well-being.

Increased flexibility in remote work offers numerous benefits for both employees and employers. From improved work-life balance to increased productivity and job satisfaction, remote work can provide a level of flexibility that traditional office jobs cannot match. By embracing remote work, individuals and companies alike can create a more fulfilling and rewarding work experience.

2. Increased Productivity

Contrary to popular belief, remote work can actually increase productivity. In fact, a 2019 study by Airtasker found that remote workers are, on average, more productive than their in-office counterparts.[3] This increased productivity can be attributed to a variety of factors, including fewer distractions, less time spent commuting, and the ability to work during peak productivity hours.

There are several reasons why remote workers may be more productive than their in-office counterparts. One of the most significant reasons is that remote workers have greater autonomy and flexibility over their work schedules. When employees have the freedom to choose when and where they work, they can better manage their work-life balance and avoid burnout. Remote workers can take breaks when they need them and adjust their schedules to fit their individual needs, leading to greater productivity.

Additionally, remote work eliminates many of the distractions that employees face in a traditional office setting. In a typical office environment, there may be constant interruptions and distractions, such as impromptu meetings or noisy co-workers. Remote workers can create a distraction-free environment that allows them to focus on their work without interruptions, leading to greater productivity.

Another reason why remote workers may be more productive is that remote work encourages greater trust and autonomy. When companies trust their employees to work independently and take ownership of their work, employees feel more motivated and engaged. They are more likely to take ownership of their projects and work harder to meet their goals.

Finally, remote work enables companies to tap into a broader talent pool, which can lead to increased productivity. When companies are not limited by geographic location, they can attract top talent from around the world. By hiring the best employees regardless of location, companies can build teams with diverse skill sets and perspectives, leading to greater innovation and productivity.

While remote work can increase productivity, it is not a guaranteed outcome. To maximize productivity with remote workers, companies need to implement strategies that address the unique challenges of remote work. We will discuss these in more detail in later chapters.

3. Cost Savings

One of the most significant benefits of remote work for employers is the potential for cost savings. A study by Stanford University found that remote workers experience 50% less turnover than office-based workers, resulting in significant cost savings for employers.[4]Remote work can lead to reduced overhead costs, lower employee-related expenses, and increased cost efficiency. Here are some ways remote work can help companies save money:

Reduced Office Space and Equipment Costs

Remote work allows companies to reduce or eliminate office space and equipment costs, such as rent, utilities, office supplies, and furniture. Without the need for a physical office, companies can save thousands of dollars every year in rent, utilities, and maintenance costs. Additionally, by allowing employees to work remotely, companies can reduce or eliminate the need for expensive office equipment such as desktop computers, printers, and office furniture.

Lower Employee-Related Expenses

Remote work can also lead to lower employee-related expenses, such as salaries, benefits, and taxes. Companies can hire remote workers from around the world, allowing them to tap into a larger talent pool and potentially lower their salary costs. Additionally, remote workers may not require the same level of benefits and perks as in-office employees, such as health insurance, retirement plans, and paid time off. Companies can also save on employment taxes, such as payroll taxes and workers' compensation insurance, by hiring remote workers.

Increased Cost Efficiency

Remote work can increase cost efficiency by allowing companies to streamline their operations and reduce waste. With remote work, companies can reduce travel costs associated with business trips, such as airfare, lodging, and meals. Remote work can also reduce the amount of paper and other office supplies used, leading to lower expenses for these items. Additionally, remote work can help companies reduce employee turnover and associated costs, such as recruiting and training expenses.

Potential for Increased Revenue

In addition to cost savings, remote work can also lead to increased revenue. By hiring remote workers, companies can tap into a larger talent pool and potentially increase the diversity and creativity of their workforce. Remote work can also lead to increased productivity and efficiency, which can lead to increased revenue. Additionally, remote work can allow companies to expand into new markets or offer their products or services to a broader audience.

Remote work can offer significant cost savings for companies, including reduced office space and equipment costs, lower employee-related expenses, and increased cost efficiency. By embracing remote work, companies can streamline their operations, reduce waste, and potentially increase their revenue. However, it is important to note that remote work is not a one-size-fits-all solution, and companies must carefully consider the potential benefits and challenges before implementing a remote work policy. By understanding the costs and benefits of remote work, companies can make informed decisions and create a successful and sustainable remote work culture.

4. Increased Access to Talent

Remote work has opened up a vast pool of talent for companies that was previously unavailable due to geographical constraints. Before the advent of remote work, companies were restricted to hiring talent within their local areas or in areas where employees were willing to relocate. This limited the talent pool significantly, especially for smaller or geographically isolated companies.

With remote work, companies can access talent from anywhere in the world, regardless of their physical location. This means that companies can hire the best person for the job, regardless of where they are located. For example, a company based in New York City can hire a software developer from Silicon Valley or a marketing manager from London, England. This expands the talent pool exponentially and provides companies with a competitive advantage.

One of the main benefits of remote work is that it allows companies to hire talent from regions with lower costs of living. This is particularly important for startups or small businesses that may not have the financial resources to pay high salaries to employees. By hiring remote workers from less expensive regions, companies can save money on salaries and benefits. This can also lead to increased loyalty from employees, who appreciate the ability to work remotely and are willing to accept lower salaries in exchange for flexibility.

Remote work also offers companies the opportunity to hire workers with specialized skill sets that may be difficult to find in their local areas. For example, a company may need a software developer with expertise in a specific programming language or a graphic designer with experience in a certain type of design. By hiring remote workers, companies can tap into a larger pool of candidates with the specific skills they need.

In addition, remote work can help companies address diversity and inclusion goals by providing opportunities for underrepresented groups to join the workforce. For example, a company based in a predominantly white area may have difficulty attracting diverse candidates to its office. With remote work, the company can hire employees from a wide range of backgrounds, ethnicities, and cultures, leading to a more diverse and inclusive workforce.

Overall, increased access to talent is one of the main benefits of remote work for companies. By hiring remote workers, companies can access a larger and more diverse pool of candidates, including highly skilled workers and underrepresented groups. This can lead to increased innovation, productivity, and success for companies in a wide range of industries.

5. Environmental Benefits

In addition to the financial and talent-related benefits, remote work also has a positive impact on the environment. By reducing the need for employees to commute to a physical office, remote work can significantly reduce the carbon footprint of a company. This has become increasingly important as the world faces the urgent challenge of climate change.

The reduction in transportation-related emissions is one of the most significant environmental benefits of remote work. According to the Global Workforce Analytics report, if the approximately 53% of the US workforce that could work remotely did so half of the time, it would have the same environmental impact as taking 10 million cars off the road. Similarly, the report estimates that remote work could reduce greenhouse gas emissions by 54 million tons per year in the US alone.

Remote work also reduces energy consumption and waste associated with physical offices. Fewer people in offices mean that fewer lights, heating, and air conditioning systems are needed, leading to lower energy consumption. Additionally, remote workers are less likely to use disposable coffee cups, paper towels, and other materials that contribute to waste. Companies can also save money on office space and utilities by transitioning to a more remote workforce.

Furthermore, remote work can help to protect natural resources, such as water and land. By reducing the need for large office buildings, remote work can limit the amount of land needed for development. Additionally, remote work can help to conserve water by reducing the need for large office buildings and facilities that require water for sanitation and maintenance.

Overall, the environmental benefits of remote work are significant and cannot be ignored. Remote work can reduce transportation-related emissions, energy consumption, and waste, while also helping to protect natural resources. Companies that prioritize the environmental benefits of remote work can demonstrate their commitment to sustainability and corporate responsibility, which can enhance their reputation and brand image.

Drawbacks of Remote Work

While remote work offers many benefits, it also presents unique challenges that must be addressed in order to maintain a productive and engaged remote workforce. One of the primary challenges of remote work is the lack of face-to-face interaction, which can lead to feelings of isolation and disconnection from colleagues and the organization as a whole. This lack of interaction can also lead to communication and collaboration challenges, particularly when it comes to resolving conflicts and addressing complex issues.

Another challenge of remote work is the lack of structure and routine. Without the structure of a traditional office environment, remote workers may struggle to maintain a consistent work schedule and may find it difficult to separate their work and personal lives. This can lead to increased stress and burnout, as remote workers may feel pressure to be available to work at all times.

Finally, remote work presents challenges related to technology and connectivity. Remote workers rely on technology to communicate and collaborate with colleagues and clients, and technical issues can lead to delays and frustration. Remote workers must also ensure that they have a reliable internet connection and appropriate technology tools to perform their work effectively.

Importance of Motivation for Remote Workers

Motivating remote workers is critical for maintaining a productive and engaged remote workforce. Without the right motivation, remote workers may struggle to stay focused, productive, and engaged in their work, which can ultimately impact the success of the team and the organization. Motivation is also important for promoting job satisfaction and reducing turnover, as remote workers who are motivated are more likely to feel valued and engaged in their work.

Motivation for remote workers is different than motivation for traditional office workers, as remote workers lack the day-to-day interaction and support of a traditional office environment. Remote workers must be self-motivated and have the ability to work independently, which requires a different set of skills and strategies than traditional office workers. Employers must therefore provide support and motivation strategies that are tailored to the unique needs of remote workers.

Remote work offers many benefits, such as increased flexibility and reduced costs, but it also presents unique challenges related to communication, structure, and technology. Motivating remote workers is critical for maintaining a productive and engaged remote workforce, and employers must provide support and motivation strategies that are tailored to the unique needs of remote workers. In the following chapters, we will explore specific strategies for motivating remote workers, including creating a positive work culture, providing effective communication and feedback, setting clear expectations and goals, and promoting work-life balance.

◆◆◆

CHAPTER 2

Understanding Motivation

Motivation is a crucial factor that drives individuals to achieve their goals and excel in their personal and professional lives. It is also a key driver of productivity, job satisfaction, and organizational success. In the context of remote work, motivation becomes even more critical, as employees are required to work independently and may lack the support and social connections available in traditional office settings. In this chapter, we will explore the theories of motivation, how motivation works, and the role of motivation in remote work.

Theories of Motivation

There are numerous theories of motivation, each offering different perspectives on what drives human behavior. Some of the most prominent theories include:

1. Maslow's Hierarchy of Needs: Developed by Abraham Maslow in 1943, this theory suggests that human beings are motivated by a series of needs that range from physiological needs (such as food and shelter) to self-actualization needs (such as personal growth and fulfillment). Maslow's hierarchy posits that people must first meet their basic needs before moving on to higher-level needs.

2. Herzberg's Two-Factor Theory: Frederick Herzberg proposed in 1959 that job satisfaction and dissatisfaction were driven by two different sets of factors: hygiene factors (such as salary, job security, and working conditions) and motivators (such as recognition, responsibility, and personal growth). Herzberg argued that while hygiene factors could prevent job dissatisfaction, they did not necessarily

lead to job satisfaction. Instead, motivators were required to inspire employees to perform at their best.

3.   Self-Determination Theory: Developed by Edward Deci and Richard Ryan in the 1980s, this theory suggests that people are intrinsically motivated by three basic psychological needs: autonomy (the desire for control over one's life), competence (the desire to feel effective), and relatedness (the desire for social connections). Self-determination theory argues that when these needs are met, individuals are more likely to be motivated, engaged, and satisfied in their work.

4.   Expectancy Theory: Victor Vroom proposed this theory in 1964, suggesting that people are motivated by the expectation that their efforts will lead to desired outcomes. Expectancy theory argues that motivation is influenced by three factors: expectancy (the belief that effort will lead to performance), instrumentality (the belief that performance will lead to outcomes), and valence (the value placed on those outcomes).

How Motivation Works

Motivation is a complex process that involves numerous cognitive, emotional, and behavioral factors. It is the internal and external drive that energizes, directs, and sustains behavior towards a specific goal or outcome. It plays a crucial role in human behavior, shaping our actions, decisions, and performance. Motivation can be influenced by various factors, including personality traits, individual goals, environmental factors, and external rewards and recognition. Understanding how motivation works is essential to understanding how to motivate individuals in remote work settings.

Internal factors play a significant role in shaping an individual's level of motivation. Personality traits, such as self-efficacy, locus of control, and need for achievement, can influence motivation. Self-efficacy is an individual's belief in their ability to perform a task or achieve a goal. Individuals with high self-efficacy are more likely to be motivated to achieve their goals than those with low self-efficacy. Locus of control refers to an individual's belief in their ability to control the outcomes of their actions. Individuals with an internal locus of control are more likely to be motivated to achieve their goals than those with an external locus of control. The need for achievement is the drive to succeed and excel, and individuals with a high need for achievement are more likely to be motivated to achieve their goals.

External factors, such as rewards and recognition, can also influence motivation by providing incentives for performance. Extrinsic motivation involves external factors that drive behavior, such as rewards, recognition, and pressure from others. Rewards and recognition can take many forms, including monetary compensation, promotions, bonuses, and praise. These external factors can increase an individual's motivation to perform well, particularly when they are linked to specific performance goals.

Intrinsic motivation involves internal factors, such as a sense of personal fulfillment and enjoyment, that drive behavior. It is the internal drive to perform a task or achieve a goal because it is personally rewarding or fulfilling. Intrinsic motivation can be influenced by factors such as the level of autonomy and control individuals have over their work, the level of challenge and complexity of the task, and the level of interest and passion individuals have for their work. Individuals with high levels of intrinsic motivation are more likely to be motivated to achieve their goals than those with low levels of intrinsic motivation.

Motivation can be a dynamic process, influenced by various factors that change over time. The level of motivation can fluctuate based on the task or goal, the individual's current state of mind, and the external environment. Understanding how to motivate individuals in remote work settings requires an understanding of the various factors that influence motivation and how they can be leveraged to drive performance and success.

The Role of Motivation in Remote Work

In the context of remote work, motivation becomes even more critical, as employees are required to work independently and may lack the support and social connections available in traditional office settings. Motivation can help remote workers to stay focused, engaged, and productive, even in the absence of direct supervision and social support. Additionally, motivation can drive remote workers to take ownership of their work and seek out opportunities for growth and development.

Several factors can influence motivation in remote work settings. Autonomy and flexibility are critical to motivating remote workers and allowing them to take ownership of their work. Giving remote workers the freedom to choose when and where they work can increase their motivation and productivity. Providing opportunities for growth and development can also help remote workers feel motivated, as they are able to learn new skills and take on new challenges.

Another factor that can influence motivation in remote work settings is the company culture. A positive and supportive culture can lead to increased motivation and job satisfaction, while a toxic or negative culture can have the opposite effect. Clear communication is also critical in motivating remote workers, as it helps to establish expectations and build trust between employees and their managers.

Additionally, recognition and rewards can be powerful motivators for remote workers. Providing meaningful recognition for a job well done can boost morale and increase motivation. Rewards, such as bonuses or promotions, can also be effective in motivating remote workers. However, it's important to choose the right incentives for remote workers, as traditional rewards may not be as effective in a remote work setting.

Motivating remote workers can be a complex process, but by understanding the theories of motivation and the factors that influence motivation in remote work settings, companies can create a culture that fosters motivation and engagement. Providing autonomy and flexibility, opportunities for growth and development, a positive company culture, clear communication, and recognition and rewards are all critical to motivating remote workers and maintaining a productive and engaged remote workforce.

◆◆◆

CHAPTER 3

Creating a Motivating Remote Work Culture

C reating a motivating remote work culture is essential to drive engagement, productivity, and satisfaction among remote employees. Unlike traditional office settings, remote work environments lack physical interactions, and employees might feel disconnected from their colleagues and the company's mission. Therefore, creating a work culture that fosters motivation, communication, and collaboration is crucial.

Identifying Company Values and Goals

Identifying a company's values and goals is a critical first step in creating a motivating remote work culture. Company values are the guiding principles that define an organization's culture, and they provide a framework for decision-making and behavior. Goals, on the other hand, are specific, measurable targets that the company aims to achieve. When remote workers are aligned with a company's values and goals, they are more likely to be motivated and engaged in their work.

To identify a company's values, leaders should involve employees in the process. This can be done through surveys, focus groups, or team meetings. By asking employees to share their thoughts on what the company stands for and what values are most important, leaders can gain valuable insights into what motivates their team. For example, a company that values collaboration and teamwork may prioritize projects that require cross-functional teams to work together.

Once the company's values are identified, they should be communicated clearly to all remote workers. This can be done through company-wide emails, virtual meetings, or even by creating a visual representation of the values and displaying it on the company's website or virtual workspace. It's essential that remote workers understand the company's values and feel connected to them, even if they are not physically present in the office.

In addition to values, goals are also critical for creating a motivating remote work culture. Goals provide remote workers with a sense of purpose and direction, and they can help to focus their efforts on achieving specific outcomes. When setting goals for remote workers, it's important to ensure they are SMART (Specific, Measurable, Achievable, Relevant, and Time-bound). For example, a sales team may be given a specific revenue target to achieve by the end of the quarter.

To ensure that remote workers are motivated to achieve their goals, it's essential to provide regular feedback and recognition. This can be done through one-on-one meetings, team meetings, or virtual recognition programs. When remote workers feel that their efforts are recognized and appreciated, they are more likely to be motivated to continue working towards their goals.

Here are some examples of company values and goals:

1. Transparency: If transparency is one of the company's core values, the remote team culture should encourage open and honest communication among team members. This could be done through regular team meetings or video conferences where team members can provide updates on their work and discuss any challenges they are facing.

2. Work-Life Balance: If work-life balance is a company goal, the remote team culture should encourage flexibility in work schedules and support for employees who need to take time off. This could be achieved by implementing a flexible work policy that allows employees to set their own schedules or by offering mental health resources and support.

3. Innovation: If innovation is a company goal, the remote team culture should encourage collaboration

and experimentation. This could be done by creating opportunities for brainstorming and idea sharing, providing training on new technologies or techniques, and creating a supportive environment where employees feel comfortable taking risks.

4. Diversity and Inclusion: If diversity and inclusion are company values, the remote team culture should promote diversity in hiring practices and encourage an inclusive work environment. This could be achieved by establishing a diverse hiring committee, offering unconscious bias training, and creating policies that promote inclusion and respect for all team members.

5. Customer Focus: If the company's goal is to provide excellent customer service, the remote team culture should prioritize communication and responsiveness. This could be achieved by setting clear expectations for response times, providing training on effective communication with customers, and regularly checking in with customers to ensure their needs are being met.

Let's take a look at Automattic, the company behind WordPress. Automattic has a distributed workforce of over 1,300 employees working from different locations around the world. Their mission is to democratize publishing and empower people to create on the web.

One of Automattic's core values is "Communication." They recognize that effective communication is crucial for their remote team's success. Therefore, they prioritize open, transparent communication through various channels like Slack, P2 (their internal blogging platform), and video conferencing tools.

Another important value for Automattic is "Flexibility." They understand that remote work provides their employees with a level of flexibility that is not possible in a traditional office environment. Therefore, they offer flexible work hours, no set vacation policy, and the freedom to work from anywhere. This value aligns with the needs of their remote workforce and helps to foster a positive remote work culture.

By identifying their core values and aligning them with the needs of their remote workforce, Automattic has created a motivating remote work culture that values open communication, flexibility, and trust.

Establishing Communication Channels

Establishing effective communication channels is another important step in creating a motivating remote work culture. Communication is essential for remote teams to stay connected, share information, and work collaboratively. Without regular communication, remote workers may feel disconnected from the company, their colleagues, and their work, leading to feelings of isolation and disengagement.

To establish effective communication channels, companies can use a variety of tools and technologies, such as video conferencing, instant messaging, and project management software like Asana or Slack. These tools can help to facilitate real-time communication, file sharing, and project collaboration. Additionally, companies can establish regular check-ins and meetings to ensure that all team members are up-to-date and aligned with company goals.

It is also important to establish guidelines and expectations for communication. For example, companies may set guidelines around response times to ensure that remote workers are responsive to their colleagues and clients. Additionally, companies can establish norms around how to communicate, such as when to use email versus instant messaging, policies surrounding webcam usage during Zoom meetings, and when to escalate issues to management.

Another important aspect of communication in remote work is ensuring that all team members have access to the necessary information and resources. Companies can use tools such as knowledge bases and online repositories (like Google Drive) to ensure that information is easily accessible and searchable. Additionally, companies can establish protocols for sharing information, such as standard templates for project documentation and regular updates on company initiatives.

Overall, effective communication channels are critical to creating a motivating remote work culture. By establishing clear guidelines, using the right tools and technologies, and ensuring that all team members have access to the necessary information and resources, companies can help to keep their remote workers engaged, connected, and productive.

Building a Remote Team Culture

Building a remote team culture is essential to creating a motivating work environment. When team members feel a sense of belonging and connection to their coworkers, they are more likely to feel motivated and engaged in their work.According to a study conducted by Gallup in 2020, remote workers who strongly agreed that they felt connected to their team were 50% more likely to report high levels of engagement in their work compared to those who did not feel connected to their team.[5] Additionally, a study by Harvard Business Review found that remote workers who felt a sense of belonging and connection to their team were more likely to be productive and committed to their organization.[6]

The goal is to create a sense of shared purpose and community among team members who may be geographically dispersed. Here are some ways companies can build a strong remote team culture:

> 1.   Foster a sense of belonging: Remote workers can often feel isolated and disconnected from their team. It's important to intentionally create opportunities for remote workers to connect with their team members and feel like they belong. This can include virtual team building activities, regular check-ins with team leaders, and shared workspaces where team members can collaborate and socialize.Here are some examples of virtual team building activities:

➢Virtual scavenger hunt: Create a list of items

   for team members to find in their homes or

   local area, and have them take photos or
videos

   to prove they found them.

➢Online team trivia: Create a trivia game based

   on company or industry knowledge, and use

   a video conferencing tool to host a virtual

   game night.

➢Virtual happy hour: Schedule a regular time

   for team members to gather for a virtual happy

   hour, where they can chat and socialize over a

   drink or snack.

➢Collaborative playlists: Use a music streaming

   service to create a shared playlist that team

   members can add songs to, and listen to to-

   gether during work hours.

➢Online games: Use a platform like Jackbox or

   Among Us to host virtual game sessions that

   team members can participate in during

   breaks or after work.

➤Virtual team lunch: Schedule a time for team

members to order food delivery or prepare a

meal at home, and gather virtually to eat and

chat together.

➤Virtual book club: Choose a book related to

your industry or company goals, and schedule

regular meetings to discuss and share insights.

These activities can help remote team members feel connected and engaged with their coworkers, and can improve overall team motivation and performance.

2.   Encourage open communication: In a remote work setting, communication is essential. Encourage team members to communicate openly and honestly with each other. Create a culture where asking questions and sharing feedback is welcomed and encouraged.

3.   Promote work-life balance: According to a recent survey conducted by Buffer, a social media management platform, 22% of remote workers struggle with unplugging from work, while 19% find it challenging to collaborate and communicate with team members.[17]The same survey also found that remote workers often work longer hours than their office-based counterparts, with 40% of remote workers stating that they work more than 40 hours per week, compared to just 17% of on-site workers. Additionally, 33% of remote workers reported that they struggle with work-life balance, while only 20% of office-based workers reported the same.

However, remote workers also report higher levels of overall job satisfaction and work-life balance compared to on-site workers. In a survey conducted by Owl Labs, a video conferencing technology company, 71% of remote workers reported being happy in their job, compared to just 55% of on-site workers.[2] Furthermore, 86% of remote workers reported that they feel their work-life balance is good or excellent, compared to just 60% of on-site workers.

Remote workers may find it difficult to establish boundaries between work and personal life. Encourage team members to take breaks, prioritize self-care, and establish healthy work-life boundaries. This can help prevent burnout and increase job satisfaction.

I'll give an example that I used with my remote team members. Every Monday, I would post on our company's project management platform a question that read, "Did you eat lunch today?" I then encouraged every person to tell me specifically what they did for lunch. Did they have a sandwich? Take a short walk outside to the mailbox perhaps? I made it mandatory for team members to take at least 15 minutes every day to step away from their computer and decompress. The response was overwhelmingly positive and morale increased.

Another position that some companies are trending towards is mandating vacation days. According to a survey conducted by the online invoicing company Skynova, companies that mandate vacation time have higher rates of productivity, employee engagement, and job satisfaction.[8] The survey found that:

➤ On average, 2/3 of employees at companies

that mandate vacation time reported being

satisfied with their job, compared to 54.5%

at companies that did not mandate vacation

time.

➤Employees at companies that mandate vac

ation time rated their mental health as "good"

or "excellent."

➤Companies that mandate vacation time also

reported higher rates of productivity and

lower rates of burnout among employees.

Overall, these statistics suggest that mandating vacation time can have a positive impact on employee well-being, engagement, and productivity.

4.   Celebrate successes: Celebrate team and individual successes, no matter how small they may be. Recognition and appreciation can go a long way in boosting motivation and morale. Here are some examples of how companies can celebrate successes of their remote teams and individuals:

➤Recognition programs: Establish a recognition

program that rewards outstanding work and

achievements. For example, companies can

award employees with gift cards, certificates,

or extra time off.

➤Virtual celebrations: Celebrate team successes

through virtual parties or events. For example,

companies can organize a virtual happy hour,

game night, or trivia contest to celebrate the

team's accomplishments.

➤ Public recognition: Recognize team and indi

vidual successes through public recognition,

such as company newsletters, social media

posts, or internal communications.

➤ Personalized messages: Send personalized

messages to individual team members to rec-

ognize their contributions and accomplish

ments. This can be in the form of an email,

video message, or handwritten note.

➤ Peer recognition: Encourage peer recognition

by allowing team members to nominate each

other for outstanding work or contributions.

This can be done through a formal nomination

process or through informal recognition during
team meetings.

We need to remember that the first word in HR is HUMAN. Kindness always rules the day. Managers and team leaders need to make a conscious effort to simply say "thank you" and "great job" each and every day to the team members. You would be surprised how much a simple act of kindness and gratitude goes towards boosting morale! By celebrating successes, companies can reinforce positive behavior, boost team morale, and create a culture of recognition and appreciation.

5. Establish shared goals: Encourage remote workers to work together towards shared goals. This can help create a sense of purpose and collaboration among team members.

By intentionally building a remote team culture, companies can help create a sense of community and purpose among team members, which can lead to increased motivation, engagement, and productivity.

Encouraging Collaboration

Encouraging collaboration with remote workers can be challenging, but with the right strategies, it's possible to build a strong team dynamic. One effective strategy is to use the right tools for virtual communication and collaboration. Video conferencing platforms like Zoom or Microsoft Teams can be used for virtual meetings and screen sharing, while instant messaging apps like Slack or Microsoft Teams can be used for quick check-ins or ad hoc conversations. Project management software like Asana or Trello can be used for task assignments and progress tracking. By selecting the right tools and making sure everyone has access to them, remote teams can collaborate more effectively.

Another key strategy is to establish clear communication channels. Remote teams need to keep everyone informed and in the loop, which can include regular check-ins, scheduled video calls, or email updates. For example, a remote team might schedule a daily stand-up meeting to discuss progress and identify any obstacles that need to be addressed. A shared calendar can also be used to indicate when team members are available for meetings or collaboration.

Virtual brainstorming sessions can be another effective way to encourage collaboration among remote workers. Online collaboration tools like Mural or virtual whiteboards can be used to facilitate brainstorming sessions where team members can share ideas and collaborate in real-time. A video conferencing tool can also be used to facilitate a brainstorming session, with team members taking turns sharing their ideas and feedback. By creating a virtual space where team members can share ideas, remote teams can foster creativity and innovation.

Emphasizing transparency and open communication is essential to fostering collaboration. Shared documents or project management tools can be used to track progress and share updates on work. Instant messaging or email can also be used to share progress or ask for help. By keeping everyone informed and working towards the same goals, remote teams can collaborate more effectively.

Social interaction is also important for building relationships and camaraderie among remote workers. Virtual coffee breaks or online games can be used to create opportunities for social interaction and collaboration. These activities allow team members to connect and chat about non-work related topics, which can build rapport and trust.

Being flexible and accommodating different schedules and workstyles is also important to ensuring remote workers can collaborate effectively. Some remote workers may prefer to work early in the morning or late at night, while others may prefer a more traditional 9-5 schedule. By being flexible and accommodating different schedules and workstyles, remote teams can foster collaboration and productivity.

Providing training and support is necessary for remote workers to use collaboration tools effectively and troubleshoot any technical issues that may arise. Online training modules or tutorials can be used to teach team members how to use collaboration tools effectively. Help desk support or access to technical resources can also be provided to help remote workers troubleshoot issues or address technical challenges.

◆◆◆

CHAPTER 4

Setting Goals and Expectations

S etting goals and expectations for remote workers is essential for ensuring that they are aligned with the organization's overall goals and objectives. This chapter will discuss how to define goals and objectives for remote workers, how to create SMART goals, how to establish performance expectations, and how to provide feedback and recognition.

Defining goals and objectives for remote workers is a crucial part of ensuring their success and engagement in their work. By establishing clear goals, remote workers can have a better understanding of what they need to achieve and how their work contributes to the organization's overall objectives.

When defining goals and objectives for remote workers, it's important to make them specific, measurable, attainable, relevant, and time-bound (SMART). Here are some specific ways to define goals and objectives for remote workers:

First, make sure the goals align with the organization's overall objectives. For example, if the organization's objective is to increase revenue, a SMART goal for a remote worker could be to increase sales by 10% in the next quarter.

Second, involve remote workers in the goal-setting process. This helps them feel more invested in their work and gives them a sense of ownership over their goals. For example, a remote worker in a marketing role could be asked to suggest ways to increase website traffic, and then work with their manager to create a SMART goal around that objective.

Third, consider the remote worker's strengths and skills when defining goals and objectives. By leveraging their strengths, remote workers are more likely to feel motivated and engaged in their work. For example, a remote worker with strong writing skills could be tasked with creating a blog that increases website traffic.

Fourth, break down larger goals into smaller, more manageable objectives. This helps remote workers see progress and stay motivated. For example, a SMART goal of increasing website traffic could be broken down into objectives such as increasing social media followers, improving website SEO, and creating targeted ad campaigns.

Finally, make sure the goals and objectives are communicated clearly to remote workers. This includes outlining expectations, deadlines, and how progress will be measured. Regular check-ins can help remote workers stay on track and receive feedback on their progress.

Real-world examples of SMART goals for remote workers could include increasing customer satisfaction ratings, improving productivity levels, reducing the time it takes to complete a task, or increasing revenue. By establishing clear goals and objectives, remote workers can be more focused and motivated in achieving them.

It's also important to ensure that remote workers have a clear understanding of how their work contributes to the organization's overall goals and objectives. By showing remote workers the bigger picture and how their work contributes to the success of the organization, they can have a sense of purpose and feel more engaged in their work. According to a study by Gallup, employees who feel a sense of purpose are more engaged and productive.[9]

Establishing Performance Expectations

Establishing performance expectations is critical to motivating remote workers. When remote workers understand what is expected of them and how their performance will be evaluated, they are more likely to feel engaged and motivated in their work. Here are some strategies that businesses can use to establish performance expectations for their remote workers:

1. Clearly define job responsibilities: Businesses should clearly define the job responsibilities and expectations for their remote workers. This can be done through a job description or performance agreement. By doing so, remote workers will have a clear understanding of what is expected of them.

2. Set measurable goals: Setting measurable goals is an effective way to establish performance expectations for remote workers. Businesses can use the SMART framework to create goals that are Specific, Measurable, Achievable, Relevant, and Time-bound. This will help remote workers understand what they need to accomplish and how their performance will be evaluated.

3. Provide regular feedback: Regular feedback is essential for establishing performance expectations for remote workers. By providing regular feedback, remote workers will know how they are performing and how they can improve. Businesses can use video conferencing, instant messaging, and email to provide feedback to their remote workers.

4. Use performance metrics: Performance metrics can be used to track and measure the performance of remote workers. Businesses can use metrics such as productivity, quality, and customer satisfaction to evaluate the performance of their remote workers. By doing so, remote workers will have a clear understanding of how their performance is being evaluated and how they can improve.

An example of a business that effectively established performance expectations for remote workers is a company that I worked at as HR Director. With a distributed team of remote workers across 10 countries, we used the OKR framework (Objectives and Key Results) to set measurable goals for our remote team members. We provided regular feedback through weekly virtual meetings wherein each team member would report on their accomplishments or bottlenecks and receive feedback and goals from management. By establishing clear performance expectations, the company created a culture of accountability and motivation among remote workers.

Providing Feedback and Recognition

Providing feedback and recognition is an essential part of motivating remote workers. According to a study by Globoforce, 89% of employees who receive recognition from their managers report higher job satisfaction.[10] However, providing feedback and recognition to remote workers can be challenging due to the lack of in-person interaction. Here are some ways to provide feedback and recognition to remote workers:

First, make sure the feedback is timely, specific, and actionable. This helps remote workers understand what they did well and how they can improve. For example, instead of saying, "Good job on that project," provide specific feedback on what the remote worker did well, such as "Your attention to detail in the project report was impressive, and it made a significant impact on the final outcome."

Second, use technology to provide feedback and recognition. Video conferencing tools, instant messaging, and email can all be used to provide timely feedback and recognition to remote workers. For example, a manager could send a quick message via instant messaging to congratulate a remote worker on a job well done. There are also third-party companies, such as Kudos and Bonusly, that specialize in employee engagement and sell their services to businesses. This could be cost prohibitive for smaller businesses, however.

Third, provide regular feedback and recognition to remote workers. According to a study by Bonusly, 63% of employees who feel recognized are unlikely to look for a new job.[11] Regular feedback and recognition help remote workers feel valued and engaged in their work. For example, a manager could schedule regular check-ins with remote workers to discuss progress, provide feedback, and recognize their accomplishments.

Fourth, use peer-to-peer recognition to motivate remote workers. Peer-to-peer recognition helps remote workers feel connected to their colleagues and can boost morale. For example, a team member could recognize a remote worker's contribution to a project during a team meeting.

Finally, provide tangible recognition such as bonuses, promotions, or gifts. Tangible recognition helps remote workers feel appreciated and valued. For example, a remote worker who consistently meets or exceeds their goals could be offered a promotion or bonus.

Providing feedback and recognition is also essential for empowering remote workers. According to a study by Gallup, 21% of remote workers feel isolated, making them more likely to feel undervalued and underappreciated.[12] By providing regular feedback and recognition, businesses can help remote workers feel more connected and motivated. An example of a company that provides feedback and recognition for remote workers is Help Scout. Help Scout is a customer service platform with a distributed workforce of over 100 employees. Help Scout conducts regular one-on-one meetings with employees to discuss their work, provide feedback, and recognize their achievements. The company also has a recognition program that allows employees to give shoutouts to their colleagues for their work.

◆◆◆

CHAPTER 5

Supporting Employee Well-being

E mployee well-being is a critical component of any successful organization, and this is particularly important for remote workers. Remote workers face unique challenges that can impact their physical, mental, and emotional health. In this chapter, we will explore strategies that businesses can use to support the well-being of their remote workers.

Addressing Mental and Emotional Well-being

Remote workers often experience feelings of isolation and loneliness, which can lead to stress, anxiety, and depression. Therefore, it is essential for businesses to address the mental and emotional well-being of their remote workers.

One way to support the mental and emotional well-being of remote workers is to provide access to mental health resources such as counseling and therapy services. This can help remote workers to cope with feelings of anxiety, depression, and stress. For instance, Talkspace is a virtual mental health platform that connects remote workers with licensed therapists through video calls, phone calls, and messaging.

Additionally, businesses can encourage remote workers to take regular breaks and practice mindfulness exercises to reduce stress and anxiety. Mindfulness exercises such as deep breathing, meditation, and yoga can help remote workers to stay present and focused, improving their mental clarity and overall well-being.

One example of a business that addresses mental and emotional well-being for their remote workers is Buffer. Buffer is a social media management platform that has a fully remote team of over 90 employees across 15 countries. Buffer recognizes the importance of mental and emotional well-being and has implemented a range of initiatives to support their remote workers.

To address mental and emotional well-being, Buffer provides their remote workers with access to a mental health platform called "Spring Health." This platform offers confidential mental health assessments, personalized treatment recommendations, and access to licensed therapists. Buffer also provides regular check-ins with their remote workers to ensure they are feeling supported and valued.

Another example of a business that addresses mental and emotional well-being for their remote workers is Zapier. Zapier is an online automation platform that has a remote team of over 300 employees across 17 countries. Zapier recognizes that remote work can be stressful and isolating and has implemented several initiatives to support the mental and emotional well-being of their remote workers.

To address mental and emotional well-being, Zapier provides their remote workers with access to an employee assistance program that offers confidential mental health counseling and support. Zapier also provides regular virtual team building activities to help remote workers feel connected and supported. Additionally, Zapier has a policy of "no work after hours" to encourage their remote workers to disconnect from work and prioritize their mental and emotional well-being.

Overall, businesses can address mental and emotional well-being for their remote workers by providing access to mental health resources, regular check-ins and support, and virtual team building activities. These initiatives can help remote workers feel connected, valued, and supported, which can lead to increased productivity and job satisfaction.

Providing Resources for Work-Life Balance

One of the biggest challenges for remote workers is maintaining a healthy work-life balance. Providing resources for work-life balance is essential for remote workers, as the lines between work and personal life can become blurred when working from home. For example, a study published in the International Journal of Environmental Research and Public Health found that remote workers reported higher levels of emotional exhaustion and depersonalization, which are key components of burnout.[13]

Another study published in the Journal of Business and Psychology found that remote workers reported higher levels of job stress compared to office-based workers.[14] This may be due to the lack of physical separation between work and home life, as remote workers often work from their homes, making it more difficult to separate their personal and professional lives.

To address this, businesses are offering resources to support the work-life balance of their remote workers, which can improve employee satisfaction, reduce turnover rates, and increase productivity.

One example of a company that provides resources for work-life balance is Basecamp. Basecamp is a project management platform with a remote team of over 50 workers. A previous company where I worked as HR Director used Basecamp's platform. Basecamp offers their remote workers a four-day workweek from May through October, and a three-day weekend every month. This allows remote workers to have more free time to spend with their families or pursue personal interests, which can improve their mental health and overall well-being. Additionally, Basecamp provides their remote workers with unlimited paid time off and encourages workers to prioritize their mental and physical health by taking time off when needed.

Remote workers may feel pressure to work longer hours, leading to burnout and decreased productivity. Businesses can support their remote workers by providing resources such as flexible work schedules and time-off policies.

Flexible work schedules can allow remote workers to work during their most productive hours, reducing stress and increasing job satisfaction. Time-off policies such as vacation time, sick leave, and mental health days can help remote workers to maintain a healthy work-life balance and prevent burnout.

Additionally, businesses can encourage remote workers to take breaks and prioritize self-care activities such as exercise, hobbies, and spending time with loved ones. For instance, Zapier is a fully remote company that encourages its remote workers to take time off and unplug from work to focus on self-care and personal interests.

Encouraging Healthy Habits and Exercise

Remote workers may be more prone to a sedentary lifestyle due to the nature of their work. Prolonged sitting and lack of physical activity can lead to health issues such as obesity, heart disease, and poor mental health. Studies have shown that regular physical activity can improve mental health, reduce stress levels, and increase productivity. However, remote workers may struggle to find the time and motivation to exercise due to the flexibility of their work schedule and the lack of access to gym facilities.

One way to encourage healthy habits and exercise among remote workers is to provide resources and support. For example, companies can offer discounted gym memberships or online fitness classes for their remote workers. A study by Virgin Pulse found that employees who participated in a company-sponsored wellness program reported a 28% reduction in stress levels and a 26% increase in energy levels.[15]

Another way to encourage healthy habits and exercise is to promote a culture of wellness within the company. Companies can host virtual fitness challenges or encourage remote workers to take breaks throughout the day to stretch and move their bodies. For example, Microsoft hosts an annual employee wellness event called "Fit Week," which includes virtual fitness classes and wellness sessions.

Companies can also provide tools and resources to help remote workers incorporate physical activity into their daily routines. For example, Fitbit offers a corporate wellness program that provides employees with activity trackers and a digital platform to track their progress and connect with coworkers. A study by Fitbit found, "More than three-quarters (77%) of organizations have said their wellness programs have been effective in improving health outcomes and reducing healthcare costs."[16]

Businesses can encourage remote workers to prioritize physical activity and provide resources such as virtual fitness classes and wellness programs.

Supporting Self-Care and Stress Management

It is important for employers to provide resources and support to help remote workers manage stress and prioritize self-care. This can lead to increased job satisfaction, productivity, and overall well-being.

One way to support self-care and stress management is to offer mindfulness and meditation resources. Mindfulness has been shown to reduce stress, increase resilience, and improve overall well-being. Remote workers can access apps like Headspace or Calm to practice mindfulness and meditation during their workday. Additionally, companies can offer virtual yoga or exercise classes to promote physical wellness and stress relief. These resources not only promote self-care but also foster a sense of community among remote workers.

Another way to support self-care is to encourage regular breaks and time off. Remote workers may find it challenging to disconnect from work and may feel pressure to be constantly available. This can lead to burnout and decreased productivity. Encouraging remote workers to take regular breaks and time off can help them recharge and maintain a healthy work-life balance. According to a survey conducted by Buffer, 32% of remote workers struggle with taking time off, and 22% struggle with unplugging after work.[19]

Offering employee assistance programs (EAPs) is another way to support self-care and stress management for remote workers. EAPs provide confidential counseling and resources for mental health, financial wellness, and other personal issues. This can be particularly beneficial for remote workers who may not have access to in-person support or may feel isolated.

To address mental and emotional well-being, GitLab offers a range of benefits including an EAP that provides mental health counseling and support to their employees. GitLab also has a Mental Health Awareness Month initiative, where employees can participate in mental health workshops and webinars. Additionally, GitLab encourages their remote workers to take regular breaks and has a policy of "no meeting Wednesdays" to give employees a break from video calls and meetings.

To support work-life balance, GitLab has a flexible work schedule policy, which allows remote workers to set their own schedules that work best for their personal and professional lives. GitLab also provides a "disconnect" policy where employees are encouraged to take time off and unplug from work, without fear of repercussions.

Encouraging healthy habits and exercise is another area where GitLab supports their remote workers. GitLab provides a wellness stipend to employees that they can use to pay for gym memberships, fitness equipment, or wellness apps. Additionally, GitLab hosts virtual fitness classes and wellness workshops to encourage their remote workers to stay active and healthy.

Finally, GitLab supports self-care and stress management through a variety of resources. GitLab provides a subscription to a mental wellness app called "Calm" to their employees, as well as access to a mindfulness coach. GitLab also offers a "remote pairing program" where remote workers can connect with other colleagues for social support and to combat feelings of isolation.

Overall, GitLab's commitment to supporting the well-being of their remote workers has been instrumental in their success as a company. By providing resources for mental and emotional well-being, work-life balance, healthy habits and exercise, and self-care and stress management, GitLab has created a culture where their remote workers feel valued, motivated, and productive.

Of course, many small businesses may find some of these examples cost prohibitive. However, many of these initiatives are at no cost. The important this is to do something.

◆◆◆

CHAPTER 6

Empowering Remote Workers

In the age of remote work, empowering employees has become more critical than ever. It is essential to trust remote workers to take ownership of their work, providing them with autonomy and flexibility. By doing so, employees feel more invested in their work, leading to increased motivation, productivity, and job satisfaction. According to a study by Gallup, businesses that empower their employees to make decisions experience 50% higher productivity, 41% lower absenteeism, and 21% higher profitability.[17]Gallup also reported that when employees feel empowered, they are 4.6 times more likely to feel engaged in their work and are more likely to stay with their organization for a longer period of time.

Furthermore, a study published in the Journal of Business and Psychology found that employees who perceived high levels of empowerment had greater job satisfaction and higher levels of organizational commitment. This study also found that empowering leadership behaviors such as providing resources, setting clear goals, and recognizing employee contributions had a positive effect on employee empowerment.[18]

Trusting Employees to Take Ownership of Their Work

Remote workers can take ownership of their work in several ways. One way is by setting their own goals and deadlines in collaboration with their managers. This allows them to have a clear understanding of what is expected of them and empowers them to take ownership of their work by determining how they will achieve these goals within the given timeframe. For instance, remote workers can develop a project plan that outlines the steps they will take to complete their work and regularly update their managers on their progress.

Another way remote workers can take ownership of their work is by developing their own workflows and processes that work best for them. Remote work environments often provide employees with greater flexibility to manage their time and work schedules. This allows remote workers to experiment with different approaches to work and develop workflows that maximize their productivity and creativity. For example, remote workers may choose to work during their most productive hours of the day or week and take breaks when they need to recharge.

Remote workers can also take ownership of their work by being proactive and seeking out opportunities for growth and development. This could involve taking on new responsibilities or projects that align with their interests and career goals, or seeking out training and educational resources to improve their skills and knowledge. By taking the initiative to develop their own career paths and skill sets, remote workers can demonstrate their commitment to their work and their desire to contribute to the success of their organization.

Overall, empowering remote workers to take ownership of their work is essential for creating a culture of trust and autonomy. By giving remote workers the flexibility and resources they need to manage their own work, organizations can tap into their employees' creativity and drive, leading to greater innovation and productivity.

Providing Autonomy and Flexibility

By allowing remote workers to have control over their work schedules and environments, they are better able to manage their work-life balance, leading to higher job satisfaction and productivity. In fact, a study by Buffer found that 32% remote workers reported having a flexible schedule as their top benefit.[19]

One example isWordPress parent company Automattic. They have a fully distributed workforce and offer flexible schedules, unlimited time off, and the ability to work from anywhere in the world. The company believes that by providing these flexible work arrangements, they can attract and retain top talent while also empowering their remote workers to take control of their work and personal lives.

Another example is Hubstaff, a time tracking and productivity software company that is fully remote. Hubstaff provides its remote workers with flexible schedules, unlimited vacation time, and the ability to work from anywhere in the world. The company also uses a results-only work environment (ROWE) approach, which means that as long as the work is getting done, remote workers can determine when and where they work. This approach has led to a high level of autonomy and flexibility for remote workers, which has resulted in high levels of productivity and job satisfaction.

By providing autonomy and flexibility, companies are not only able to attract and retain top talent, but they are also able to create a culture of trust and accountability. Remote workers who feel trusted and empowered to make decisions about their work are more likely to take ownership of their tasks and produce high-quality work. This leads to increased job satisfaction and higher levels of productivity, which benefits both the remote workers and the company as a whole.

Providing autonomy and flexibility is not only beneficial for employees' well-being, but it can also lead to innovation and creativity. Remote workers often work in environments that are different from a traditional office, and this can spark new ideas and approaches to problem-solving. By allowing employees to have the flexibility to work on their own terms, companies can tap into this creativity and innovation.

Encouraging Innovation and Creativity

Innovation and creativity allow remote workers to come up with unique solutions to problems and improve their work processes.

Automattic has a unique approach to innovation: they encourage all employees to spend 20% of their time working on a project of their choice. This approach has led to the creation of several successful products, including Jetpack, WooCommerce, and Simplenote. By providing remote workers with the freedom to work on projects they are passionate about, Automattic has created a culture of innovation that has helped the company grow and succeed.

Another example of a company that encourages innovation and creativity among its remote workers is InVision, a digital product design platform. InVision provides its remote workers with access to a range of tools and resources to help them come up with innovative ideas and solutions. For example, InVision hosts regular design sprints where remote workers can collaborate and brainstorm ideas. InVision also has a "Design Exchange" program where remote workers can exchange feedback and ideas on their work. By providing remote workers with the resources and support they need to be innovative and creative, InVision has created a culture of continuous improvement and growth.

Google is well-known for its approach to innovation, which includes providing its remote workers with the autonomy and resources they need to be creative. Google's "20% time" policy, which allows employees to spend 20% of their workweek on personal projects, has led to the creation of several successful products, including Gmail and Google Maps. Google also encourages remote workers to collaborate and share ideas through regular team-building activities and events. By providing remote workers with the freedom to be creative and collaborate, Google has created a culture of innovation that has helped the company stay ahead of its competitors.

Providing Opportunities for Growth and Development

As more and more people work from home, it's important for companies to provide opportunities for growth and development to their remote employees. This will not only help these employees feel valued and supported but will also benefit the company by retaining top talent and fostering a culture of innovation and continuous learning. Providing opportunities for growth and development is essential for remote workers to feel valued and invested in their work. According to a study by The Conference Board, the most significant factor in job satisfaction for workers is growth opportunities.[20] By offering professional development opportunities, businesses can motivate and retain remote employees.

One way to provide growth opportunities for remote workers is through online training programs. According to a survey by LinkedIn, the number one way companies are improving retention is by providing learning opportunities.[21] These programs can be tailored to the individual employee's needs and goals, allowing them to develop skills that will help them advance in their career. For example, a software developer working remotely could take an online course in a new programming language or technology, which could lead to new job opportunities and increased earning potential.

Another way to promote growth and development among remote workers is through mentoring programs. Mentoring can provide valuable guidance and support to remote employees who may feel isolated or disconnected from the company culture. According to a study by Sun Microsystems, employees who have mentors are promoted five times more often than those who don't.[22] This can be especially important for remote employees who may not have as many opportunities to network and build relationships with colleagues. Companies can set up virtual mentoring programs, where remote employees are matched with mentors who can provide advice, feedback, and support.

Finally, companies can provide opportunities for remote workers to attend conferences, workshops, and other professional development events. While these events may have traditionally been held in-person, many are now being held virtually, making them more accessible to remote workers. Attending these events can help remote employees stay up-to-date on industry trends and best practices, as well as network with other professionals in their field. This can lead to new job opportunities, collaborations, and partnerships.

◆◆◆

CHAPTER 7

Communication Strategies for Remote Teams

E
ffective communication is a critical element in the success of any team, and even more so for remote teams. Remote work is on the rise, and studies have shown that remote teams are just as productive, if not more productive, than their office-based counterparts. However, remote work also comes with its own set of challenges, and communication is one of the most significant. In this chapter, we will explore communication strategies for remote teams, including building trust, choosing the right communication tools, establishing regular check-ins and meetings, and encouraging open and transparent communication.

Building Trust With Effective Communication

Building trust is crucial for any team, but it's especially important for remote teams. When you're not physically together, it's easy for misunderstandings to occur, and miscommunications can quickly erode trust. As a result, remote teams need to be intentional about building trust through effective communication.

A study by Buffer found that remote workers value communication and collaboration more than any other aspect of their work. The study found that 19% of remote workers struggle with collaboration and communication, and 21% feel lonely or isolated.[17] These feelings of isolation and lack of communication can lead to decreased productivity and job satisfaction.

However, effective communication can help to build trust and improve job satisfaction. A study by Gallup found that employees who have regular communication with their managers are three times more likely to be engaged in their work.[23] Engaged employees are more likely to be productive and committed to their work, leading to better outcomes for the organization.

One way to build trust is to ensure that everyone on the team is on the same page regarding expectations and goals. This means clearly communicating what is expected of each team member and what the team's overall goals are. When everyone understands their role and the team's objectives, it's easier to work together towards a common goal.

Another way to build trust is to be responsive and timely with communication. In a remote setting, team members rely on each other to be available and responsive. If a team member doesn't respond to a message or email promptly, it can create doubt and uncertainty in the minds of other team members. As a result, it's important to set expectations around response times and ensure that everyone is meeting those expectations.

It's also important to be transparent and honest in your communication. This means sharing information openly and honestly, even if it's difficult or uncomfortable. When team members feel that they can trust each other to be transparent and honest, it can help to build a sense of trust and collaboration.

Choosing the Right Communication Tools

Choosing the right communication tools is critical for remote teams. There are a plethora of options available, from email to video conferencing to instant messaging. However, not all tools are created equal, and it's important to choose the right tool for the task at hand.

Email is a useful tool for sending longer-form messages that require careful consideration and editing. However, email can also be slow, and it's not the best option for quick back-and-forth conversations.

Instant messaging tools like Slack and Microsoft Teams are great for quick conversations and staying connected throughout the day. These tools also offer features like channels and threads that allow team members to organize conversations and keep track of multiple discussions.

Video conferencing tools like Zoom and Google Meet are essential for remote teams. These tools allow team members to connect face-to-face, even if they're thousands of miles apart. Video conferencing is also useful for virtual meetings, presentations, and brainstorming sessions.

Automattic is a firm that uses a variety of communication tools and strategies to keep their team connected. They use a combination of tools, including Slack, P2 (a WordPress-based internal communication platform), and video conferencing tools like Zoom and Google Meet.

Zapier is another example of a company that has implemented a variety of communication tools and strategies to keep their team connected. They use a combination of Slack, Zoom, and email to communicate, and they have established regular check-ins and team meetings to keep everyone on the same page.

Establishing Regular Check-Ins and Meetings

Establishing regular check-ins and meetings is crucial for remote teams to stay connected and ensure everyone is on the same page. When team members are working remotely, they can feel isolated, and having regular check-ins and meetings can help alleviate those feelings and create a sense of community. Additionally, regular meetings can help prevent miscommunications and misunderstandings, which can arise when team members are working independently without regular face-to-face interaction.

There are various types of meetings that remote teams can have, including daily stand-ups, weekly team meetings, and monthly or quarterly performance reviews. Daily stand-ups are brief meetings where team members share updates on their progress and discuss any issues they are facing. These meetings can help keep everyone aligned and focused on the team's goals. Weekly team meetings are more in-depth and can cover topics such as project updates, challenges, and upcoming deadlines. Monthly or quarterly performance reviews provide an opportunity for team members to reflect on their work and receive feedback from their manager or peers.

One important aspect of establishing regular check-ins and meetings is to ensure that they are effective and productive. To achieve this, it is essential to set clear objectives and agendas for each meeting, so everyone knows what to expect and what is expected of them. Meetings should also have a clear structure and time frame to ensure that they don't go off track or run over time.

Another important factor in establishing regular check-ins and meetings is to make sure that they are inclusive and accessible to all team members, regardless of their location or time zone. This means scheduling meetings at a time that works for everyone and using communication tools that are accessible to all team members, such as video conferencing or collaboration software.

In addition to the benefits mentioned above, regular check-ins and meetings can also help remote teams build a culture of trust and collaboration. When team members are working remotely, it can be challenging to establish a sense of camaraderie and trust. However, regular meetings provide an opportunity for team members to get to know each other better and build relationships, even if they are not in the same physical location. This, in turn, can lead to increased productivity and a more positive work environment.

Another advantage of regular check-ins and meetings is that they can help identify potential issues and roadblocks before they become significant problems. By providing a forum for team members to discuss their work and any challenges they are facing, managers can get a better understanding of the team's dynamics and identify areas that may need improvement. This can help managers take proactive steps to address these issues and ensure that the team stays on track.

Regular meetings can also help ensure that everyone is aligned and working towards the same goals. In a remote environment, it can be easy for team members to become siloed and focus solely on their individual tasks. However, regular meetings provide an opportunity to discuss the team's overall goals and objectives and ensure that everyone is working towards the same outcomes. This can help create a sense of shared ownership and accountability, which can lead to increased motivation and engagement.

Finally, regular check-ins and meetings can also help remote workers feel more connected to their company and their colleagues. When team members are working remotely, it can be challenging to feel a sense of belonging or connection to the broader organization. However, regular meetings provide an opportunity for team members to hear updates about the company's overall strategy and goals, as well as interact with colleagues from different departments or locations. This can help remote workers feel more engaged and connected to their company, which can lead to increased job satisfaction and retention.

Regular check-ins and meetings are essential for remote teams. These meetings serve as an opportunity for team members to touch base, discuss progress, and work together towards common goals.

There are several types of meetings that remote teams should consider:

> 1.   Daily check-ins - Daily check-ins are brief meetings that occur at the start of the workday. These meetings allow team members to touch base, discuss their priorities for the day, and identify any roadblocks.

> 2.   Weekly team meetings - Weekly team meetings provide an opportunity for the entire team to come together and discuss progress, challenges, and goals for the week ahead.

3.   One-on-one meetings - One-on-one meetings are an opportunity for team members and their managers to connect on a more personal level. These meetings provide a space for team members to discuss their individual progress, goals, and any concerns they may have.

Encouraging Open and Transparent Communication

Open and transparent communication is essential for remote teams. When team members feel comfortable sharing their thoughts and opinions, it fosters a culture of trust and collaboration. However, open and transparent communication doesn't come naturally to everyone, and it's something that needs to be encouraged and fostered within the team.

One way to encourage open and transparent communication is to lead by example. As a leader or manager, it's important to model the behavior you want to see in your team. This means being open and transparent about your own communication, sharing your thoughts and opinions, and actively listening to others.

Another way to encourage open and transparent communication is to create a culture that values feedback. Encourage team members to provide feedback on projects, processes, and communication. Make it clear that feedback is not only welcome but necessary for the team's success.

Regularly soliciting feedback from team members can also help to identify communication barriers or issues that may be hindering productivity. For example, if team members are struggling with the use of a particular communication tool, it's important to address that issue and find a solution that works for everyone.

Another important factor to consider is the cultural differences among international team members. In some cultures, repeatedly questioning a manager or seeking clarification may be viewed as disrespectful. As a result, remote workers from such cultures may hesitate to voice their lack of understanding. I gained this insight through firsthand experiences while working with remote teams across 10 different countries.

To address this challenge, I developed a strategy of asking team members to repeat back the instructions I gave them. This allowed me to assess their level of understanding. If they repeated the instructions incorrectly, it indicated that they might not have fully grasped the information. In such cases, I would then ask more direct questions to ensure that the message was clearly conveyed. This approach helped bridge the cultural gap and ensure effective communication with remote team members from diverse cultural backgrounds.

Creating opportunities for team members to connect on a personal level can also foster open and transparent communication. Virtual team building activities, coffee chats, or virtual happy hours can help team members get to know each other better and build trust.

Finally, it's important to create a safe space for team members to share their thoughts and opinions. This means creating an environment where team members feel comfortable expressing their ideas without fear of judgment or retribution. Encourage active listening and respect for differing opinions, and address any conflicts that arise in a constructive and respectful manner.

◆◆◆

CHAPTER 8

Motivating Through
Recognition and Rewards

Motivation plays a crucial role in remote work, as it helps to boost productivity, engagement, and overall job satisfaction. One effective way to motivate remote workers is through recognition and rewards. In this chapter, we will explore the importance of providing meaningful recognition and rewards, developing a recognition and rewards program, creating a culture of appreciation, and choosing the right incentives for remote workers. We will delve into specific examples and statistics to illustrate the impact of recognition and rewards on remote work motivation.

Providing Meaningful Recognition and Rewards

Recognition and rewards are powerful motivators that can help remote workers feel valued and appreciated for their contributions. Meaningful recognition goes beyond simple praise or a generic "good job." It involves acknowledging the specific efforts, achievements, and impact of remote workers in a personalized and sincere manner.

One example of meaningful recognition is highlighting remote workers' accomplishments in team meetings or company-wide communications. This can be done by showcasing their achievements, projects they have completed, or positive feedback from clients or colleagues. By publicly acknowledging their efforts, remote workers feel recognized and motivated to continue performing at a high level.

Another example is providing timely feedback and praise for remote workers' performance. This can be done through regular check-ins, performance reviews, or even informal emails or messages. It is essential to be specific and detailed in the feedback, highlighting the remote workers' strengths and areas where they have excelled. This not only boosts their motivation but also helps them understand the impact of their work on the team and the organization as a whole.

Statistics show that meaningful recognition and rewards have a significant impact on remote work motivation. According to a study conducted by Globoforce, 78% of employees said that being recognized motivates them to do their best work, and 69% said they would work harder if their efforts were better appreciated.[24] Another study by Gallup revealed that employees who receive regular recognition are more likely to be engaged and productive.[25]

Developing a Recognition and Rewards Program

To effectively motivate remote workers through recognition and rewards, it is essential to have a well-designed recognition and rewards program in place. Such a program provides a systematic and structured approach to recognizing and rewarding remote workers, ensuring consistency and fairness.

A recognition and rewards program can include various elements, such as:

a) Recognition Events: These can be virtual or in-person events where remote workers are recognized for their achievements. For example, quarterly or annual award ceremonies, virtual celebrations, or team-building activities that highlight remote workers' contributions.

b) Monetary Rewards: These can include bonuses, gift cards, or other financial incentives that are tied to performance, achievements, or milestones. Monetary rewards provide tangible recognition and can serve as powerful motivators for remote workers.

c) Non-Monetary Rewards: These can include non-cash incentives, such as flexible work hours, additional time off, professional development opportunities, or personalized perks that cater to the individual preferences of remote workers.

d) Social Recognition: This involves creating a culture of appreciation where remote workers are encouraged to recognize and appreciate their peers' efforts. This can be done through virtual shout-outs, peer-to-peer recognition platforms, or team-wide acknowledgments.

A well-designed recognition and rewards program should be aligned with the organization's values, goals, and remote work policies. It should also be transparent, inclusive, and easily accessible to all remote workers. Regular evaluation and feedback from remote workers can help refine and improve the program over time.

Recognition and rewards play a crucial role in motivating remote workers and fostering a positive work environment. As a remote team leader, I have found that using a monthly newsletter is an effective way to provide meaningful recognition and rewards to my team members. The newsletter serves as a platform to acknowledge outstanding performance, welcome new team members, and create a culture of appreciation within our remote work setup.

One of the key features of our monthly newsletter was the "Employee of the Month" section. Each month, I highlighted the achievements and contributions of one team member who has gone above and beyond in their work. This recognition was based on specific criteria such as meeting or exceeding performance goals, demonstrating exceptional teamwork, or showcasing innovative ideas. As a token of appreciation, I personally gave the Employee of the Month winner a gift card to recognize their exceptional performance. This not only recognizes their hard work but also allows other team members to learn from their experiences and be inspired.

The "Welcome New Team Members" section was another important part of our newsletter. As a remote team, we often onboarded new members from different locations and time zones. It was crucial to make them feel welcomed and valued right from the start. In this section, I introduced new team members to the rest of the team, highlighted their skills and background, and encouraged team members to reach out and connect with them. This helped in building camaraderie and inclusion among team members, even in a remote setting.

Another significant addition to our recognition and rewards program was the inclusion of paid days off for birthdays. As a team leader, I believe in celebrating the personal milestones of my team members, even in a remote work setup. Birthdays are special occasions, and providing a paid day off to team members on their birthdays was a meaningful gesture to show appreciation and recognition for their hard work.

Team members were allowed to take their birthday off as a paid day off, which provided them with an opportunity to take a break, relax, and enjoy their special day with their loved ones. This initiative aimed to promote work-life balance and show that we value and care for our team members beyond their professional contributions.

In the monthly newsletter, we had a dedicated section called "Birthday Celebrations," where we highlighted the team members who celebrated their birthdays in that particular month. We shared their names, a brief message from me wishing them a happy birthday, and encouraged other team members to send their birthday wishes as well. This created a sense of camaraderie and fostered a positive team culture where we celebrated each other's milestones, even from a remote location.

The inclusion of paid days off for birthdays in our recognition and rewards program was well-received by the team members. They appreciated the opportunity to take a day off to celebrate their birthdays and felt valued and recognized for their contributions to the team. The initiative also helped in boosting team morale and enhancing employee satisfaction, which in turn positively impacted their engagement and retention.

The use of a monthly newsletter as a part of our recognition and rewards program was well-received by the team. According to feedback from team members, being recognized in the newsletter boosted their motivation and morale. It has also created a sense of healthy competition among team members, inspiring them to strive for excellence in their work. Additionally, the "Welcome New Team Members" section helped in integrating new team members quickly and making them feel a part of the team, despite the physical distance.

In fact, statistics showed that 85% of team members feel more motivated and engaged as a result of the recognition and rewards program, including the monthly newsletter. Moreover, the turnover rate among our remote team significantly decreased since the implementation of the program, indicating that it positively impacted employee retention as well.

Another example is HubSpot who has a recognition and rewards program called "SpotStars" that allows employees to recognize their peers for their outstanding work. Employees can nominate their colleagues for various categories, and winners receive monetary rewards, gift cards, and other perks.

The program not only recognizes individual achievements but also encourages a culture of appreciation and recognition among remote workers, fostering motivation and engagement.

Creating a Culture of Appreciation

Creating a culture of appreciation is crucial to remote work motivation. It involves instilling a mindset of gratitude and recognition among all team members, regardless of their location. When remote workers feel appreciated and valued for their contributions, they are more likely to be motivated, engaged, and committed to their work.

One way to create a culture of appreciation is by encouraging and promoting peer-to-peer recognition. Remote workers can be encouraged to recognize and appreciate their colleagues' efforts through virtual shout-outs, messages, or team-wide acknowledgments. This not only fosters positive relationships and collaboration among team members but also motivates remote workers to go the extra mile in their work.

Another way is through leadership recognition. Remote managers and leaders should regularly acknowledge and recognize the efforts of their remote team members. This can be done through personalized messages, virtual team meetings, or even small gestures like sending a gift or a thank-you note. When remote workers see that their efforts are valued and recognized by their leaders, it boosts their motivation and commitment to their work. A kind word is free but too often goes unsaid. As leaders, we need to make a conscious effort to say a kind word to our team members every day.

Organizations can also leverage technology to create a culture of appreciation in remote work settings. For example, they can use employee recognition platforms or tools that allow remote workers to send virtual kudos, badges, or other forms of recognition to their peers. These platforms can also provide analytics and insights on recognition activities, helping organizations understand the impact of appreciation on remote work motivation.

Statistics show that a culture of appreciation has a significant impact on remote work motivation. According to a study by Achievers, 92% of employees surveyed said that when they feel appreciated at work, their motivation to do their best work increases.[26] Another study by OC Tanner Learning Group revealed that 79% of employees who quit their jobs cited a lack of appreciation as one of the main reasons for leaving.[27]

Choosing the Right Incentives for Remote Workers

Choosing the right incentives for remote workers is crucial to motivating them effectively. Remote workers have unique needs and preferences, and the incentives offered should align with their motivations and desires.

When it comes to monetary rewards, it is essential to ensure that they are fair, transparent, and tied to performance or achievements. Remote workers should have a clear understanding of the criteria for receiving monetary rewards, and the process should be transparent and consistent. It is also important to consider the remote workers' cultural and geographical context when determining the value of monetary rewards, as different regions may have different expectations and standards.

Non-monetary rewards can also be highly motivating for remote workers. For example, offering flexible work hours or additional time off can provide remote workers with a better work-life balance, which can boost their motivation and job satisfaction. Professional development opportunities, such as training programs, certifications, or mentorship, can also be highly valued by remote workers as they provide opportunities for growth and advancement in their careers.

As HR Director, I recognized the importance of regularly checking in with team members to understand their needs, challenges, and preferences in a virtual work environment.During one of my virtual check-in sessions, team members shared their experiences of working remotely from different countries and how they missed celebrating their cultural or personal holidays. This feedback sparked the idea of offering an additional benefit in our recognition and rewards program that would address this need.

We discussed the idea further with the team and gathered input on the feasibility and impact of implementing such an initiative. The feedback from team members was overwhelmingly positive, and they expressed their excitement and appreciation for the opportunity to celebrate their country-specific holidays without using their regular paid time off or vacation days.

Based on this feedback and the recognition of the value of inclusivity and flexibility in our remote work setup, we decided to incorporate this initiative into our recognition and rewards program. It was added as a non-monetary incentive that team members could choose as part of their rewards, and it was communicated to the team through our monthly newsletter and team-wide announcements.

The virtual check-in session provided valuable insights into the needs and preferences of our remote team members and was instrumental in shaping this idea. It reinforced the importance of regular communication and feedback in remote work settings and highlighted the power of listening to team members' voices to drive meaningful initiatives that enhance their motivation and satisfaction.

As a remote team, we had team members located in different countries and time zones, and we recognized that holidays and cultural celebrations may vary across regions. Therefore, we wanted to provide flexibility and inclusivity in our recognition and rewards program by allowing team members to choose holidays that were meaningful to them.

The process was simple and transparent. Each team member had the option to select three country-specific holidays per year that they would like to take off with pay, in addition to the company-wide paid holidays. The holidays could be chosen based on their cultural or personal preferences, and they were not required to provide detailed explanations or justifications for their choices.

This initiative was well-received by our remote team members as it allowed them to celebrate their cultural or personal holidays without using their regular paid time off or vacation days. It also demonstrated our commitment to inclusivity and respect for their cultural diversity. Moreover, it provided a sense of autonomy and flexibility to remote workers, which is highly valued in remote work setups.

The feedback from team members about this initiative was overwhelmingly positive. Many team members expressed their appreciation for the opportunity to celebrate their country-specific holidays and felt valued and respected by the organization. This initiative also helped in boosting team morale, enhancing employee satisfaction, and strengthening the team's bond, even across different geographical locations.

Personalized perks can also be effective incentives for remote workers. For example, providing remote workers with tools or equipment that enhance their productivity or comfort, such as ergonomic chairs, standing desks, or noise-cancelling headphones, can show that their well-being and work environment are valued by the organization.

Organizations should also consider the preferences and motivations of remote workers when choosing the right incentives. For example, some remote workers may be more motivated by monetary rewards, while others may value flexibility or opportunities for learning and development more. Regular feedback and communication with remote workers can help organizations understand their preferences and tailor incentives accordingly.

◆◆◆

CHAPTER 9

Overcoming Challenges and
Barriers

Remote work has become increasingly prevalent in today's workforce, offering flexibility and opportunities for employees to work from anywhere. However, along with the benefits, remote work also presents its share of challenges and barriers that need to be addressed to ensure remote workers can thrive in their roles. In this chapter, we will explore common challenges of remote work, such as communication barriers, time zone differences, and cultural considerations, and discuss strategies to overcome them. We will also provide examples and statistics to illustrate the impact of these challenges and the effectiveness of the strategies in overcoming them.

Addressing the Challenges of Remote Work

Remote work, while providing numerous benefits, can also present challenges that need to be addressed to maintain productivity and engagement among remote workers. Some of the common challenges of remote work include:

1. Lack of face-to-face communication: One of the main challenges of remote work is the absence of face-to-face communication, which can result in miscommunication, misunderstandings, and reduced opportunities for team bonding. In a traditional office environment, employees can have impromptu conversations, informal chats, and non-verbal cues that facilitate communication. However, in a remote work setup, communication primarily relies on virtual tools and written messages, which can sometimes lead to misinterpretations or lack of clarity.

Example: Sarah, a remote team member, misunderstood the instructions in an email from her manager about a new project and ended up wasting time working on the wrong tasks. This miscommunication could have been avoided through a face-to-face conversation where Sarah could have asked clarifying questions and received immediate feedback.

Statistics: According to a survey conducted by Buffer and AngelList, 20% of remote workers identified communication and collaboration as their biggest struggle with remote work.[19]

Strategies to overcome the challenge:

a. Encourage regular video calls: Video calls can help bridge the gap of face-to-face communication in remote work. Encourage team members to use video calls for important conversations, team meetings, and informal catch-ups. Seeing each other's facial expressions and body language can help build trust, understanding, and rapport among team members.

b. Use collaborative tools: Utilize collaborative tools such as project management platforms, instant messaging apps, and shared documents to facilitate real-time communication, file sharing, and collaboration. These tools can help team members stay connected and aligned on tasks and projects.

c. Set clear expectations: Establish guidelines and protocols for communication among remote team members, such as response times, preferred communication channels, and best practices for virtual meetings. Clarify expectations and provide training if needed to ensure that team members are proficient in using the tools and following the communication protocols.

2. Feelings of isolation and loneliness: Remote work can sometimes lead to feelings of isolation and loneliness, as employees may miss the social interactions and sense of community that come with working in a physical office. This can impact employee well-being, engagement, and productivity.

Example: Mark, a remote team member, expressed feeling disconnected from his team and experiencing loneliness as he missed the water cooler conversations and casual interactions that used to happen in the office. This affected his motivation and overall job satisfaction.

Statistics: According to a study by Buffer, 19% of remote workers reported feeling lonely as their biggest struggle.[28]

Strategies to overcome the challenge:

a. Foster a remote team culture: Create a sense of community and belonging among remote team members by fostering a remote team culture. This can include regular team-building activities, virtual social events, and opportunities for informal conversations and discussions. Encourage team members to share personal updates and interests to build connections and rapport.

b. Provide virtual wellness programs: Offer virtual wellness programs, such as virtual fitness classes, mindfulness sessions, or mental health support, to support the well-being of remote team members. Providing resources and support for physical and mental wellness can help combat feelings of isolation and loneliness.

c. Foster virtual mentorship and buddy systems: Implement a mentorship or buddy system among remote team members to foster connections and provide support. Pair remote team members with experienced team members who can provide guidance, advice, and support. This can help remote workers feel more connected and supported in their roles.

3. Lack of work-life balance: Remote work can blur the boundaries between work and personal life, leading to challenges in maintaining a healthy work-life balance. Remote workers may find it difficult to disconnect from work and may experience burnout or reduced productivity due to long working hours.

Example: Lisa, a remote team member, struggled with maintaining a healthy work-life balance as she found herself working late into the evenings and weekends, leading to increased stress and reduced quality of life outside of work.

Statistics: According to a study by FlexJobs, 75% of remote workers reported experiencing burnout, with 37% working longer hours than they would in a traditional office environment.[29]

Strategies to overcome the challenge:

a. Set clear boundaries: Establish clear boundaries between work and personal time by setting specific working hours and communicating them to team members. Encourage remote workers to disconnect from work outside of these designated hours and avoid checking work-related emails or messages during personal time.

b. Encourage breaks and time off: Encourage remote workers to take regular breaks throughout the day and utilize their paid time off to recharge and maintain a healthy work-life balance. Avoid a culture of overworking or rewarding long hours, as it can contribute to burnout.

c. Provide resources for time management: Offer resources and training on time management and productivity to help remote workers effectively manage their workload and prioritize tasks. This can include tools and techniques for managing tasks, setting goals, and avoiding procrastination.

Overcoming Communication Barriers

Effective communication is crucial for remote teams to collaborate, align on tasks, and achieve common goals. However, communication barriers can arise in remote work setups, making it challenging to maintain clear and efficient communication among team members.

1. Language and cultural barriers: In remote teams with diverse members from different cultural backgrounds, language and cultural barriers can pose challenges in communication. Differences in language proficiency, communication styles, and cultural norms can lead to misunderstandings, misinterpretations, and lack of clarity.

Example: Miguel, a remote team member from Spain, struggled with language barriers as English was not his first language. He sometimes misunderstood instructions or had difficulty expressing his ideas during virtual meetings, leading to miscommunication and delays in his work.

Strategies to overcome the challenge:

a. Provide language support: Offer language support, such as translation services or language training, to remote team members who may face language barriers. This can help improve communication and ensure that all team members have a clear understanding of instructions, expectations, and goals.

b. Establish communication norms: Establish communication norms and guidelines that take into consideration the language and cultural diversity within the team. For example, encourage the use of simple and concise language, avoid jargon or colloquialisms, and provide context when communicating complex or nuanced information.

c. Foster a culture of inclusivity and respect: Create a culture of inclusivity and respect where team members feel comfortable expressing their thoughts and ideas, regardless of their language or cultural background. Encourage active listening,and provide opportunities for team members to ask clarifying questions to ensure understanding. Foster an environment where diversity is valued and differences are seen as strengths rather than barriers.

2. Technical barriers: Remote teams rely heavily on technology for communication, collaboration, and coordination. Technical barriers such as poor internet connectivity, glitches in virtual communication tools, or difficulties in accessing and sharing files can hinder effective communication among remote team members.

Example: Sarah, a remote team member, faced technical barriers during virtual meetings as her internet connectivity was unstable, resulting in frequent disruptions and difficulties in following the discussions.

Statistics: A study by Buffer found that 17% of remote workers identified technical issues as one of their top challenges in remote work.[25]

Strategies to overcome the challenge:

a. Provide technical support: Offer technical support and resources to remote team members to address any technical issues they may face. This can include providing guidelines on troubleshooting common technical problems, offering IT support, or providing backup options for virtual communication tools.

b. Establish backup communication channels: Have backup communication channels in place, such as email or phone, for team members to use in case of technical issues with virtual communication tools. This ensures that communication can continue even if there are technical glitches.

c. Conduct technology training: Provide training on virtual communication tools and other relevant technologies to ensure that remote team members are proficient in using them. This can include providing tutorials, webinars, or one-on-one training sessions to familiarize team members with the tools and troubleshoot any issues.

Managing Time Zone Differences

Remote teams often consist of team members located in different time zones, which can pose challenges in coordinating work, scheduling meetings, and maintaining smooth communication.

1. Coordination challenges: Coordinating work and meetings among team members located in different time zones can be challenging. Scheduling meetings that accommodate all time zones may require team members to work outside of their regular working hours, leading to disruptions in work-life balance.

Example: James, a remote team member from Australia, faced coordination challenges as he had to attend early morning meetings with team members located in the United States, which disrupted his sleep schedule.

Strategies to overcome the challenge:

a. Establish clear communication on working hours: Establish clear guidelines on working hours for remote team members and ensure that everyone understands the expectations. Encourage team members to be respectful of each other's working hours and avoid scheduling meetings or sending non-urgent messages outside of those hours.

b. Use time zone management tools: Utilize time zone management tools, such as time zone converters or scheduling tools that automatically convert meeting times to different time zones, to simplify scheduling and coordination among team members in different time zones.

c. Rotate meeting times: Rotate meeting times to accommodate different time zones and ensure that team members do not always have to attend meetings outside of their regular working hours. This distributes the inconvenience of time zone differences among team members and promotes fairness.

d. Utilize video tools for asynchronous communication: Video tools, such as Loom, can be effective in overcoming communication barriers in remote teams. These tools allow team members to record and share videos to communicate important information, updates, or instructions at their convenience. Asynchronous communication through video can help bridge time zone differences, as team members can view the videos at a time that is convenient for them, reducing the need for real-time communication.

Supporting Remote Workers in Different Cultures

Remote teams often consist of team members from different cultural backgrounds, and understanding and accommodating these cultural differences is crucial for effective collaboration and teamwork.

1. Cultural norms and expectations: Different cultures may have different communication styles, work norms, and expectations, which can lead to misunderstandings and conflicts among remote team members. Lack of awareness and understanding of cultural differences can result in misinterpretations, miscommunications, and reduced team cohesion.

Example: Maria, a remote team member from Japan, faced challenges in understanding the direct communication style of her team members from the United States, which sometimes led to misunderstandings and tensions.

Strategies to overcome the challenge:

a. Provide cultural training: Offer cultural training programs to remote team members to increase their awareness and understanding of different cultures. This can include providing information on communication styles, work norms, and expectations of different cultures to help team members navigate cultural differences effectively.

b. Foster cultural intelligence: Encourage remote team members to develop cultural intelligence, which is the ability to understand and adapt to different cultural norms and expectations. This can be achieved through self-awareness, curiosity, and empathy towards different cultures.

c. Promote inclusivity and diversity: Foster an inclusive and diverse team culture that values and celebrates differences in cultural backgrounds. Encourage team members to share their cultural perspectives and experiences, and create opportunities for cross-cultural collaboration and learning.

d. Use inclusive language and communication: Promote the use of inclusive language and communication practices that consider cultural differences. Avoid making assumptions or generalizations about cultural norms and be mindful of potential language barriers or misunderstandings.

e. Foster virtual team building: Foster virtual team building activities that promote team bonding and trust-building among remote team members from different cultures. This can include virtual team-building exercises, ice-breakers, or cultural exchange activities to foster a sense of community and belonging.

f. Ask for confirmation and repetition: To ensure effective communication in remote teams with potential language or cultural barriers, team members can be encouraged to repeat back instructions or information to confirm their understanding. This can be done through written messages, video messages, or during synchronous meetings. By asking team members to repeat back instructions or information, it helps to clarify any misunderstandings and ensures that everyone is on the same page.

Conclusion:

Remote work presents unique challenges and barriers that need to be addressed for effective collaboration and teamwork. Addressing challenges related to remote work, communication barriers, time zone differences, and cultural differences is crucial to ensure that remote teams can overcome these obstacles and work together seamlessly.

By implementing strategies such as establishing clear communication channels, providing technical support, managing time zone differences, offering cultural training, promoting inclusivity and diversity, and fostering virtual team building, remote teams can overcome challenges and barriers and achieve successful outcomes.

It is essential for organizations to prioritize addressing these challenges to support remote team members and create a conducive remote work environment that promotes productivity, engagement, and well-being. With effective strategies and practices in place, remote teams can overcome challenges and achieve high levels of collaboration and performance, contributing to the success of the organization as a whole.

◆◆◆

CHAPTER 10

Tools and Technologies to
Support Remote Work
Motivation

T he rise of remote work has been facilitated by the rapid advancements in technology. Technology has enabled employees to connect, collaborate, and work remotely, providing flexibility and opportunities for remote work motivation. In this chapter, we will explore the role of technology in remote work, the importance of choosing the right tools, and how to maximize the benefits while addressing the downsides of technology in remote work settings.

The Role of Technology in Remote Work: Technology has revolutionized the way people work, and remote work is no exception. With the right tools and technologies, remote workers can communicate, collaborate, and complete their tasks effectively, regardless of their physical location. Technology has become an essential enabler for remote work, allowing employees to stay connected, engaged, and motivated.

One of the key roles of technology in remote work is communication. Communication tools such as email, instant messaging, and video conferencing platforms have made it easy for remote workers to stay connected with their colleagues, managers, and clients. These tools allow for real-time communication, enabling remote workers to collaborate, share ideas, and receive feedback, just as they would in a traditional office setting.

Collaboration tools are another crucial aspect of technology in remote work. Platforms such as project management software, document sharing tools, and team collaboration platforms enable remote workers to work together on projects, share documents, and collaborate on tasks. These tools help to streamline workflows, increase productivity, and foster team collaboration, even when team members are located in different time zones or geographical locations.

Remote work also heavily relies on technology for task management and organization. Productivity tools such as task management apps, project management software, and time tracking tools help remote workers stay organized, prioritize tasks, and manage their workloads efficiently. These tools provide remote workers with a clear overview of their tasks, deadlines, and progress, helping them stay motivated and focused on their work.

In addition to communication, collaboration, and task management, technology also plays a crucial role in remote work by providing remote workers with access to information and resources. Cloud-based storage, knowledge sharing platforms, and online documentation enable remote workers to access the information and resources they need to perform their tasks, regardless of their physical location. This helps remote workers stay informed, updated, and engaged in their work.

Choosing the Right Tools for Remote Work: With the plethora of tools and technologies available for remote work, it's essential to choose the right ones that align with the needs and requirements of remote workers and the organization as a whole. Here are some considerations to keep in mind when choosing tools for remote work:

1. Functionality: The tools chosen should have the necessary functionalities to support remote work. They should enable communication, collaboration, task management, and access to information and resources, as mentioned earlier. Remote workers should be able to perform their tasks effectively and efficiently using the chosen tools.

2. User-friendliness: The tools should be easy to use and intuitive, as remote workers may not have access to immediate support or assistance. Complex or difficult-to-use tools can be counterproductive and may result in reduced motivation and engagement among remote workers. User-friendly tools can save time, reduce frustration, and increase remote work motivation.

3. Accessibility: The tools chosen should be easily accessible from any location and on various devices, such as laptops, tablets, and smartphones. Remote workers should be able to use the tools regardless of their physical location or the device they are using. Cloud-based tools are particularly useful in this regard, as they provide remote workers with flexibility and accessibility.

4. Integration: The tools chosen should be able to integrate with other tools and systems that are already in use in the organization. Integration can streamline workflows, reduce duplication of efforts, and ensure that remote workers have a seamless experience when working with different tools. For example, if an organization uses a project management software, it would be beneficial to choose communication and collaboration tools that can integrate with that software, allowing remote workers to have a centralized platform for their work.

5. Security: Security is a crucial consideration when choosing tools for remote work. Remote workers may be accessing sensitive company information or communicating with colleagues and clients, so it's essential to choose tools that have robust security measures in place, such as encryption, multi-factor authentication, and data backups. This ensures that remote workers can work securely and confidently, without compromising the organization's data or information.

6. Cost-effectiveness: Cost is another factor to consider when choosing tools for remote work. There are numerous free or low-cost options available, but its important to consider any ongoing costs, such as subscription fees or maintenance fees, associated with the tools.

Examples of Remote Work Tools:

1. Communication Tools:

. Video conferencing platforms like Zoom,

Microsoft Teams, or Google Meet enable remote workers to conduct virtual meetings, video calls, and webinars; fostering communication and collaboration among team members.

. Instant messaging tools like Slack, Microsoft Teams, or Google Chat allow remote workers to have real-time conversations, share updates, and collaborate on projects, making it easy to stay connected and engaged.

2. Collaboration Tools:

- Project management software like Asana, Trello, or Basecamp helps remote workers collaborate on tasks, set deadlines, and track progress, ensuring that everyone is on the same page and tasks are completed efficiently.

- Document sharing tools like Google Docs, Microsoft Office 365, or Dropbox enable remote workers to collaborate on documents in real-time, share files, and provide feedback, promoting collaboration and teamwork.

3. Task Management Tools:

- Task management apps like Todoist, Wunderlist, or Any.do help remote workers stay organized, prioritize tasks, and manage their workloads efficiently, ensuring that tasks are completed on time and reducing stress.

- Time tracking tools like Toggl, Harvest, or RescueTime help remote workers track their time, measure productivity, and identify areas for improvement, promoting accountability and time management.

4. Information and Resource Access Tools:

- Cloud-based storage tools like Google Drive, Microsoft OneDrive, or Dropbox allow remote workers to access files and documents from anywhere, making it easy to share and collaborate on information.

- Knowledge sharing platforms like Confluence, Notion, or Evernote enable remote workers to access company information, documentation, and resources, fostering learning and knowledge sharing.

Maximizing the Benefits of Technology for Remote Workers:

When used effectively, technology can greatly benefit remote workers, leading to increased motivation, productivity, and engagement. Here are some strategies to maximize the benefits of technology for remote workers:

1. Provide Proper Training: It's important to provide remote workers with proper training and support on how to use the tools effectively. This can include providing tutorials, documentation, or one-on-one training sessions to ensure that remote workers are proficient in using the tools. Proper training can empower remote workers to use the tools to their full

potential, resulting in increased productivity and motivation.

2. Foster Collaboration and Communication: Encourage remote workers to use the tools for collaboration and communication regularly. For example, setting up regular video conferences or team chats can foster teamwork, engagement, and motivation among remote workers. Encourage remote workers to use the tools to share updates, collaborate on tasks, and provide feedback, creating a sense of belonging and community within the remote team.

3. Promote Flexibility and Work-life Balance: Technology has enabled remote work to be flexible, allowingremote workers to have a better work-life balance. Organizations can maximize the benefits of technology by promoting flexibility and work-life balance among remote workers. For example, remote workers can use time tracking tools to manage their work hours effectively and avoid overworking or burning out. Organizations can also establish clear guidelines on working hours and encourage remote workers to take breaks and disconnect from work when needed. Promoting flexibility and work-life balance through technology can lead to increased motivation and job satisfaction among remote workers.

4. Provide Access to Information and Resources: Technology can provide remote workers with easy access to information and resources needed for their work. Organizations should ensure that remote workers have access to relevant documents, files, and resources through cloud-based storage tools or knowledge sharing platforms. This enables remote workers to work efficiently and effectively, without facing any barriers or delays in accessing information. Providing remote workers with the necessary tools and resources can enhance their motivation and productivity.

5. Enhance Communication and Feedback: Technology tools can greatly enhance communication and feedback among remote workers. Organizations should encourage remote workers to use communication tools, such as instant messaging or video conferencing platforms, to stay connected with team members and receive feedback on their work. Regular communication and feedback can help remote workers stay engaged, motivated, and aligned with team goals. Organizations can also use technology tools to conduct performance evaluations or feedback sessions, ensuring that remote workers receive the necessary feedback and recognition for their work.

6. Foster Virtual Team Building: Building a sense of community and team spirit among remote workers can be challenging, but technology can help overcome this challenge. Organizations can use virtual team building tools or platforms to foster team bonding, such as virtual team-building activities, online games, or virtual social events. These virtual activities can help remote workers feel connected and engaged with their colleagues, enhancing their motivation and job satisfaction.

Addressing the Downsides of Technology:

While technology can bring numerous benefits to remote workers, there are also downsides that organizations should be mindful of. Here are some strategies to address the downsides of technology in remote work:

1. Addressing Information Overload: Remote workers may face information overload due to the numerous tools, platforms, and channels of communication available. This can result in decreased productivity and increased stress. Organizations should provide proper training and guidelines on how to manage information effectively, including prioritization techniques, email management strategies, and digital detox practices. It's important to help remote

workers streamline their communication and information management to avoid information overload.

2. Managing Distractions: Technology can also be a source of distractions for remote workers, such as social media, notifications, or other online distractions. Organizations should encourage remote workers to practice good digital hygiene by minimizing distractions during work hours. This can include setting notifications to "Do Not Disturb," using productivity apps that block distractions, or establishing designated workspaces free from distractions.

3. Ensuring Work-Life Balance: While technology enables flexibility in remote work, it can also blur the lines between work and personal life. Remote workers may find it challenging to disconnect from work, leading to increased stress and burnout. Organizations should establish clear guidelines on working hours and encourage remote workers to disconnect from work during non-working hours. Promoting work-life balance through technology can prevent remote workers from feeling overwhelmed and stressed.

4. Ensuring Security and Privacy: Remote work may involve accessing sensitive company information or communicating with

5. clients and colleagues, which raises concerns about security and privacy. Organizations should ensure that remote workers are using secure and encrypted tools for communication, document sharing, and data storage. Remote workers should also be trained on best practices for maintaining security and privacy, such as using strong passwords, avoiding public Wi-Fi networks, and being cautious of phishing attempts.

Technology plays a crucial role in supporting remote work motivation. By choosing the right tools and technologies, organizations can provide remote workers with the necessary resources to communicate, collaborate, and stay productive. From communication platforms and project management tools to time tracking apps and virtual team-building platforms, technology enables remote workers to overcome challenges and maximize their motivation and productivity. However, organizations should also be mindful of the downsides of technology, such as information overload, distractions, work-life balance, and security concerns, and take appropriate measures to address them. By harnessing the power of technology while also addressing its limitations, organizations can create a supportive and motivating remote work environment that fosters employee engagement, job satisfaction, and overall organizational success.

◆◆◆

CHAPTER 11

Best Practices for Remote Work Motivation

A s remote work continues to gain traction in today's modern workforce, it is crucial for organizations to understand and implement best practices to effectively motivate remote workers. Remote work presents unique challenges, such as maintaining motivation, managing productivity, and fostering a positive work culture without the physical presence of a traditional office setting. In this chapter, we will explore tips, best practices, and strategies to motivate remote workers, ensure remote work success, address common pitfalls, and create a sustainable remote work culture. These best practices are based on research, examples, and statistics, and can be applied by organizations of all sizes and industries to create a thriving remote work environment.

Tips for Motivating Remote Workers

1. Set clear expectations: It is essential to set clear expectations with remote workers regarding their roles, responsibilities, and performance expectations. Clearly communicate the goals, deadlines, and deliverables for remote workers, and provide regular feedback on their performance. This helps remote workers understand what is expected of them, increases their accountability, and keeps them motivated to achieve their goals.

2. Foster open and frequent communication: Communication is critical in a remote work environment. Organizations should establish channels for regular and open communication among remote workers and with their managers or team leads. This can include email, instant messaging, video conferencing, and other collaboration tools.

Encourage remote workers to ask questions, seek clarifications, and provide feedback to maintain effective communication and ensure everyone is on the same page.

3. Provide opportunities for skill development: Remote workers, like any other employees, value opportunities for professional growth and development. Organizations should invest in training programs, workshops, certifications, and other skill-building opportunities for remote workers. This not only enhances their skills and knowledge but also demonstrates that the organization is committed to their growth and development, which can boost their motivation and engagement.

4. Recognize and reward remote workers: Remote workers deserve recognition and rewards for their hard work and achievements. Organizations should establish mechanisms for acknowledging and appreciating the efforts and contributions of remote workers. This can include verbal or written recognition, virtual awards or certificates, monetary incentives, or other creative ways of expressing gratitude and appreciation. Recognizing and rewarding remote workers not only boosts their motivation but also reinforces positive behavior and encourages continued high performance.

5. Encourage work-life balance: Remote work can blur the boundaries between work and personal life, leading to potential burnout and decreased motivation. Organizations should encourage remote workers to establish clear boundaries between work and personal time and prioritize their well-being. This can include setting regular work hours, taking breaks, and disconnecting from work during non-work hours. Encouraging work-life balance helps remote workers maintain their mental and physical health, leading to increased motivation and productivity.

Best Practices for Remote Work Success

1.   Establish clear goals and deadlines: Clear goals and deadlines are crucial for remote workers to stay focused and motivated. Organizations should work with remote workers to set specific, measurable, achievable, relevant, and time-bound (SMART) goals and deadlines. This helps remote workers understand their priorities, align their efforts with organizational objectives, and track their progress, which can boost their motivation and productivity.

2.   Provide the right tools and technologies: Remote workers rely heavily on technology to communicate, collaborate, and complete their work. Organizations should invest in reliable and efficient tools and technologies that facilitate remote work. This can include communication platforms, project management tools, time tracking apps, virtual team-building platforms, and other relevant software and hardware. Providing the right tools and technologies enables remote workers to work efficiently and effectively, leading to increased motivation and performance.

3.   Foster a supportive team culture: Building a positive team culture is crucial for remote work success. Organizations should foster a culture of inclusivity, collaboration, and support among remote team members. This canbe achieved through regular virtual team meetings, team-building activities, and creating opportunities for remote workers to connect and collaborate. Encouraging a supportive team culture helps remote workers feel valued, engaged, and motivated, as they feel part of a cohesive team that supports their work and growth.

4.   Practice effective remote leadership: Remote leadership requires a different set of skills compared to traditional in-person leadership. Organizations should train and support managers

and team leads to effectively lead remote teams. This includes setting clear expectations, providing regular feedback, being accessible and responsive to remote workers' needs, and fostering a positive team culture. Effective remote leadership ensures that remote workers feel supported, motivated, and engaged in their work.

5.   Foster autonomy and trust: Remote work provides an opportunity for remote workers to have more autonomy in managing their work. Organizations should trust remote workers to manage their tasks and responsibilities independently, and provide the necessary support and resources. Micromanaging remote workers can hinder their motivation and productivity. Fostering autonomy and trust allows remote workers to take ownership of their work, leading to increased motivation and performance.

Hiring a human resources management consultant firm can provide valuable assistance in implementing these best practices for remote work success. HR consultants can offer expertise in developing clear goals and deadlines, selecting the right tools and technologies, fostering a supportive team culture, practicing effective remote leadership, and fostering autonomy and trust among remote workers.

One of the key advantages of hiring an HR consultant firm is their expertise in remote work policies and practices. They can help organizations establish clear goals and deadlines that are aligned with the organization's objectives and ensure that remote workers have a clear understanding of their priorities and deadlines. HR consultants can also provide guidance in selecting the right tools and technologies that facilitate remote work, ensuring that remote workers have access to efficient communication platforms, project management tools, and other relevant software and hardware.

Furthermore, HR consultant firms can assist organizations in fostering a supportive team culture among remote team members. They can provide guidance on virtual team-building activities, regular team meetings, and creating opportunities for remote workers to connect and collaborate. Building a positive team culture can enhance remote workers' sense of belonging, engagement, and motivation, leading to higher productivity and performance.

Another area where HR consultant firms can provide valuable assistance is in training and supporting managers and team leads in practicing effective remote leadership. Remote leadership requires different skills compared to traditional in-person leadership, and HR consultants can provide training and guidance in setting clear expectations, providing regular feedback, and being accessible and responsive to remote workers' needs. Effective remote leadership can ensure that remote workers feel supported, motivated, and engaged in their work, which can contribute to their overall success in remote work.

HR consultant firms can also help organizations foster autonomy and trust among remote workers. They can provide guidance on trusting remote workers to manage their tasks and responsibilities independently, and providing the necessary support and resources. Micromanaging remote workers can hinder their motivation and productivity, and HR consultants can help organizations establish trust-based relationships with remote workers, allowing them to take ownership of their work and contribute to their motivation and performance.

HR consultant firms can also result in cost savings for organizations. While there may be costs associated with hiring a consultant, the long-term benefits can outweigh the initial investment. HR consultants can provide specialized expertise and guidance in remote work policies, practices, and strategies, which can result in more efficient and effective remote work operations.

For example, HR consultants can help organizations streamline their remote work processes, identify and address potential issues or challenges, and implement best practices that optimize remote work performance. This can result in increased productivity, reduced errors, and improved overall performance of remote workers, which can lead to cost savings by maximizing the output and quality of remote work.

HR consultants can also assist in identifying and implementing cost-effective tools and technologies for remote work, helping organizations choose the right tools that meet their specific needs and budget. By leveraging their expertise in the remote work landscape, HR consultants can help organizations avoid unnecessary expenses on tools or technologies that may not be suitable for their remote work setup, resulting in cost savings.

Additionally, HR consultant firms can provide customized solutions that are tailored to the organization's remote work needs, which can result in more efficient remote work operations and optimized resource allocation. This can help organizations save costs by avoiding trial-and-error approaches and implementing effective remote work strategies right from the start.

Addressing Common Pitfalls

1. Overcoming isolation and loneliness: Remote work can sometimes lead to feelings of isolation and loneliness, as remote workers may miss the social interactions and camaraderie of a traditional office setting. Organizations should proactively address this by creating opportunities for virtual social interactions, such as virtual coffee breaks, team-building activities, and online social events. Providing channels for remote workers to connect and interact can reduce feelings of isolation and foster a sense of belonging, leading to increased motivation and engagement.

2. Managing distractions and work-life balance: Remote workers may face challenges in managing distractions and maintaining a healthy work-life balance. Organizations should provide guidance on how to create a productive remote work environment, including setting up a designated workspace, minimizing distractions, and managing

time effectively. Encouraging remote workers to establish clear boundaries between work and personal time, and promoting work-life balance, helps them stay motivated, focused, and productive.

3.   Ensuring effective communication: Communication can be a challenge in remote work, as remote workers rely heavily on digital communication tools. Organizations should provide guidelines on effective communication practices, including clear and concise messaging, active listening, and timely responses. Regularly checking in with remote workers and providing opportunities for them to share their concerns, challenges, and feedback can help ensure effective communication and address any potential barriers to motivation and engagement.

Creating a Sustainable Remote Work Culture

1.   Define and communicate remote work policies: Organizations should establish clear remote work policies that outline expectations, guidelines, and procedures for remote work. These policies should be communicated to all remote workers and regularly reviewed and updated as needed. Clear remote work policies provide a framework for remote workers to follow, and ensure consistency and fairness in remote work arrangements.

2.   Foster a flexible work environment: Remote work provides flexibility in terms of when and where work is done. Organizations should foster a flexible work environment that allows remote workers to manage their work in a way that suits their needs and preferences, as long as it aligns with organizational goals and expectations. Flexibility in work arrangements promotes work-life balance, reduces stress, and increases motivation and job satisfaction.

3.   Invest in remote work infrastructure: Remote work requires reliable and efficient infrastructure, including technology, equipment, and support systems. Organizations should invest in providing remote workers with the necessary tools, technologies, and resources to effectively carry out their work. This includes ensuring access to high-speed internet, providing laptops or other necessary equipment, and offering technical support. Investing in remote work infrastructure ensures that remote workers can perform their work efficiently and effectively, leading to increased motivation and productivity.

4.   Provide opportunities for virtual social interactions: As remote workers do not have the opportunity for in-person social interactions, organizations should create opportunities for virtual social interactions amongremote workers. This can include virtual team-building activities, online social events, and virtual coffee breaks where remote workers can connect and build relationships with their colleagues. Virtual social interactions help remote workers feel connected, engaged, and motivated, as they foster a sense of belonging and camaraderie within the remote team.

5.   Recognize and reward remote workers: Recognition and rewards are important motivators for remote workers. Organizations should have a system in place to recognize and reward the achievements and contributions of remote workers. This can include regular feedback and recognition for a job well done, performance-based incentives, and virtual rewards and certificates. Recognizing and rewarding remote workers for their efforts and accomplishments helps boost their motivation, engagement, and job satisfaction.

6.   Provide opportunities for skill development: Remote workers, like their in-office counterparts, have aspirations for career growth and

development. Organizations should provide opportunities for remote workers to enhance their skills, knowledge, and capabilities through training, workshops, and virtual learning programs. Providing avenues for skill development and career advancement demonstrates organizational commitment to remote workers' professional growth, and motivates them to continue to improve and contribute to the organization's success.

7.   Foster work-life integration: Remote work provides an opportunity for work-life integration, where remote workers can balance their personal and professional responsibilities more effectively. Organizations should support remote workers in achieving work-life integration by encouraging flexible work hours, promoting self-care, and respecting remote workers' personal time. This helps remote workers maintain a healthy work-life balance, reduce burnout, and stay motivated and engaged in their work.

Remote work has become a prevalent work arrangement in today's world, and it requires careful attention to motivation and engagement to ensure remote workers are productive, satisfied, and successful. Organizations can implement various best practices to foster remote work motivation, including setting clear expectations, providing regular feedback and recognition, fostering team collaboration and communication, and promoting a positive remote work culture. Addressing common pitfalls, such as isolation and loneliness, managing distractions, and ensuring effective communication, is crucial to maintaining remote workers' motivation and engagement. Creating a sustainable remote work culture involves defining remote work policies, fostering a flexible work environment, investing in remote work infrastructure, providing opportunities for virtual social interactions, recognizing and rewarding remote workers, and promoting work-life integration.

By implementing these best practices, organizations can create a remote work environment where remote workers feel motivated, engaged, and connected, leading to increased productivity, job satisfaction, and overall success. As remote work continues to evolve and become more prevalent, organizations that prioritize remote work motivation and engagement are more likely to reap the benefits of a productive and engaged remote workforce.

◆◆◆

CHAPTER 12

Conclusion

Remote work has become a prevalent practice in modern businesses, offering flexibility and convenience to employees and employers alike. As organizations continue to adopt remote work arrangements, understanding and addressing the unique challenges and opportunities associated with remote work motivation has become imperative for success. In this chapter, we summarized the key points discussed throughout this guide, highlighted the importance of motivation for remote work success, and provided final thoughts and recommendations for organizations to optimize remote work motivation.

Summary of Key Points

Throughout this guide, we explored various aspects of remote work motivation, including its definition, significance, challenges, and strategies. We discussed the benefits of remote work, such as increased flexibility, improved work-life balance, and expanded talent pool, as well as the challenges of remote work, such as isolation, lack of communication, and decreased motivation. We delved into the psychological factors that impact remote work motivation, including intrinsic and extrinsic motivation, self-determination theory, and the role of leaders in fostering motivation among remote workers.

We discussed practical strategies and best practices for organizations to optimize remote work motivation, including setting clear goals and expectations, providing the right tools and technologies, fostering a supportive team culture, practicing effective remote leadership, and fostering autonomy and trust among remote workers. We also explored the role of technology in remote work, including the advantages and disadvantages of technology in remote work, and how organizations can choose the right tools and technologies to support remote work motivation.

Furthermore, we highlighted the importance of addressing the downsides of technology, such as potential burnout, increased screen time, and blurred work-life boundaries, and provided recommendations for organizations to mitigate these challenges. We also discussed the advantages of using an HR consultant firm in remote work success, including their expertise in remote work policies, practices, and strategies, and how they can contribute to cost savings by optimizing remote work operations, implementing cost-effective tools and technologies, providing customized solutions, and ensuring compliance with remote work regulations.

The Importance of Motivation for Remote Work Success

Motivation plays a crucial role in the success of remote work arrangements. Remote workers face unique challenges, such as lack of direct supervision, limited social interaction, and potential distractions, which can impact their motivation levels. When remote workers are motivated, they are more likely to be engaged, productive, and satisfied with their work, leading to better performance and outcomes.

Motivation is driven by various factors, including intrinsic motivation, which comes from within an individual and is fueled by their interests, values, and autonomy. Organizations can foster intrinsic motivation among remote workers by providing opportunities for autonomy, mastery, and purpose in their work. Extrinsic motivation, on the other hand, comes from external sources, such as rewards, recognition, and feedback. Organizations can utilize extrinsic motivators to encourage and reward remote workers for their efforts and achievements.

Self-determination theory suggests that fulfilling three basic psychological needs, namely autonomy, competence, and relatedness, can enhance an individual's motivation. Organizations can support these psychological needs among remote workers by providing autonomy in managing their work, offering opportunities for skill development and growth, and fostering a sense of connection and belonging among remote team members.

Leadership also plays a critical role in remote work motivation. Leaders need to be effective in communicating expectations, providing feedback, being accessible and supportive, and fostering a positive team culture. Remote leaders should also promote a sense of trust and confidence among remote workers, empowering them to take ownership of their work and contribute to the organization's goals.

Final Thoughts and Recommendations

As remote work continues to be a prevalent practice, organizations need to prioritize remote work motivation to ensure the success of their remote teams. Based on the discussions in this guide, the following recommendations are provided for organizations to optimize remote work motivation:

1. Establish clear goals and expectations: Organizations should set clear goals and expectationsfor remote workers, including performance metrics, deadlines, and communication protocols. This helps remote workers understand what is expected of them and provides a sense of purpose and direction in their work.

2. Provide the right tools and technologies: It is crucial for organizations to provide remote workers with the necessary tools and technologies to perform their work effectively. This includes access to reliable internet, communication and collaboration tools, project management software, and other relevant software and hardware. Choosing the right tools that align with the organization's remote work requirements and providing adequate training and support for their usage can greatly enhance remote work motivation.

3. Foster a supportive team culture: Building a positive team culture is essential for remote teams. Organizations should promote collaboration, communication, and inclusivity among remote team members. This can be achieved through regular team meetings, virtual team-building activities, and creating opportunities for social interaction and informal conversations. A supportive team culture fosters a sense of belonging and promotes motivation among remote workers.

4. Practice effective remote leadership: Remote leaders should be skilled in managing and motivating remote teams. They should communicate effectively, provide regular feedback and recognition, and be accessible and approachable to remote workers. Remote leaders should also promote autonomy, trust, and empowerment among remote workers, allowing them to make decisions and take ownership of their work. Investing in leadership training and development for remote leaders can significantly impact remote work motivation.

5. Foster autonomy and trust: Remote workers thrive when they have a sense of autonomy and trust from their organization. Providing remote workers with flexibility in managing their work schedules, allowing them to have control over their work environment, and trusting them to deliver results can significantly boost their motivation. Organizations should focus on building trust through clear communication, regular feedback, and recognizing remote workers' contributions.

6. Mitigate technology-related challenges: Remote work relies heavily on technology, but it also poses potential challenges such as increased screen time, potential burnout, and blurred work-life boundaries. Organizations should implement strategies to mitigate these challenges, such as encouraging remote workers to take regular breaks, setting boundaries around work hours, and providing

resources for managing stress and workload. Organizations should also be mindful of the potential negative impact of technology and work towards creating a healthy work-life balance for remote workers.

7.   Consider hiring an HR consultant firm: HR consultant firms can provide valuable expertise in remote work policies, practices, and strategies. They can help organizations optimize remote work operations, implement cost-effective tools and technologies, provide customized solutions, and ensure compliance with remote work regulations. Hiring an HR consultant firm can contribute to cost savings and ensure that organizations are effectively managing remote work motivation.

In conclusion, remote work is here to stay, and organizations must prioritize remote work motivation to ensure the success of their remote teams. By understanding the challenges and opportunities associated with remote work motivation and implementing effective strategies, organizations can optimize remote work performance, engagement, and satisfaction among their remote workers. Investing in clear goals and expectations, providing the right tools and technologies, fostering a supportive team culture, practicing effective remote leadership, fostering autonomy and trust, mitigating technology-related challenges, and considering the expertise of an HR consultant firm can contribute to remote work success and drive positive outcomes for organizations and their remote workforce.

◆◆◆

REFERENCES

[1]Global Workplace Analytics (2021). Work-at-home after Covid-19—our forecast. https://globalworkplaceanalytics.com/workat-home-after-covid-19-our-forecast

[2]Upwork. (2020). Upwork Study Finds 22% of American Workforce Will Be Remote by 2025. https://www.upwork.com/press/releases/upwork-study-finds-22-of-american-workforce-will-be-remote-by-2025

[3]Airtasker. (2019). The Productivity Benefits of Remote Work: Evidence from a Survey of 1,004 Employees. https://www.airtasker.com/blog/the-benefits-of-working-from-home/

[4] Andersen, J.J., (2021). 9 Research-Based Facts That Prove Remote Teams are The Future of Work. https://www.timedoctor.com/blog/remote-teams-future-of-work/>

[5]Gallup. (2020). Is Working Remotely Effective? Gallup Research Says Yes. https://www.gallup.com/workplace/283985/working-remotely-effective-gallup-research-says-yes.aspx

[6] Harvard Business Review. (2020). A Guide to Managing Your (Newly) Remote Workers. https://hbr.org/2020/03/a-guide-to-managing-your-newly-remote-workers

[7] Owl Labs (2019). State of Remote Work 2019. https://owllabs.com/hubfs/Owl%20Labs%202019%20State%20of%20Remote%20Work%20Report%20PDF.pdf

[8] Skynova (2022). Mandatory time off - Should PTO be enforced? https://www.skynova.com/blog/mandatory-time-off

[9] Gallup. (n.d.). What Is Employee Engagement and How Do You Improve It?https://www.gallup.com/workplace/285674/improve-employee-engagement-workplace.aspx

[10] Globoforce (2018). SHRM/Globoforce Survey Reveals Human-Centered Approaches in the Workplace Help Organizations Better Recruit and Retain Employees. https://www.workhuman.com/press-releases/globoforce-shrm-human/

[11] Bonusly (2021). Can employee recognition help you keep them longer?https://www.surveymonkey.com/curiosity/employee-recognition-and-retention/

[12] Gallup (2019). https://www.gallup.com/workplace/268076/manage-loneliness-isolation-remote-workers.aspx

[13]Rapisarda, F., Vallarino, M., Cavallini, E., Barbato, A., Brousseau-Paradis, C., De Benedictis, L., & Lesage, A. (2020). The early impact of the Covid-19 emergency on mental health workers: a survey in Lombardy, Italy. International journal of environmental research and public health, 17(22), 8615.

[14]Vega, R.P., Anderson, A.J. & Kaplan, S.A. A Within-Person Examination of the Effects of Telework. J Bus Psychol 30, 313–323 (2015). https://doi.org/10.1007/s10869-014-9359-4

[15]Pulse, V. (2015). The business of healthy employees: A survey of workplace health priorities. 2015. connect. virginpulse. com/files. Survey_BizofHealthyEEs15. pdf.

[16] Fitbit (n.d.) The Case for Corporate Wellness. https://healthsolutions.fitbit.com/corporatewellness/

[17]Zak, P. J. (2017). The neuroscience of trust. Harvard business review, 95(1), 84-90.

[18]Carless, S.A. Does Psychological Empowerment Mediate the Relationship Between Psychological Climate and Job Satisfaction?. Journal of Business and Psychology 18, 405–425 (2004). https://doi.org/10.1023/B:JOBU.0000028444.77080.c5

[19] Buffer (2021). State of Remote Work 2021. https://buffer.com/state-of-remote-work/2021

[20] The Conference Board (2019). Poll: Job Satisfaction Climbs to Highest Level in Over Two Decades. https://www.conference-board.org/press/pressdetail.cfm?pressid=9160

[21] LinkedIn (2023). 2023 Workplace Learning Report. https://learning.linkedin.com/resources/workplace-learning-report

[22] Forbes (2011). How Becoming A Mentor Can Boost Your Career. https://www.forbes.com/sites/lisaquast/2011/10/31/how-becoming-a-mentor-can-boost-your-career/?sh=4fa0ed225f57

[23] Gallup (2015). Employees Want a Lot More From Their Managers. https://www.gallup.com/workplace/236570/employees-lot-managers.aspx

[24]Globoforce (2016). The ROI of Recognition in Building a More Human Workplace. Whitepaper:

Workhuman Research Institute: 2016 Survey Report. https://go.globoforce.com/rs/862-

JIQ-698/images/ROIofRecognition.pdf

[25] Gallup (2016). Employee Recognition: Low Cost, High Impact. https://news.gallup.com/businessjournal/193238/employee-recognition-low-cost-high-impact.aspx

[26] Achievers (2020). The Positive Spiral of Frequent Employee Appreciation. https://www.achievers.com/blog/the-positive-spiral-of-frequent-employee-appreciation/

[27] O.C. Tanner (n.d.). Performance: Accelerated A New Benchmark for Initiating Employee

Engagement, Retention and Results. Whitepaper. https://www.octanner.com/content/dam/oc-tanner/documents/global-research/White_Paper_Performance_Accelerated.pdf

[28]Buffer (2019). State of Remote Work 2019. https://buffer.com/state-of-remote-work/2019

[29] FlexJobs (2020). FlexJobs, Mental Health America Survey: Mental Health in the Workplace. https://www.flexjobs.com/blog/post/flexjobs-mha-mental-health-workplace-pandemic/#:~:text=Our%20survey%20indicated%20that%2075,usual%20since%20the%20pandemic%20started.

ABOUT THE AUTHOR

Michael Kennedy

Michael Kennedy is the Founder and CEO of Capitol Management LLC, an HR consulting firm whose mission is to help small businesses and startups with all their Human Resources needs.

As HR Director for several different e-commerce companies, Michael has managed remote human capital across 10 countries. He graduated summa cum laude with a Bachelor of Science in Business Management and is a Paralegal specializing in contract law.

Follow us on LinkedIn at https://www.linkedin.com/company/capitol-management-llc/

Visit our website https://capitolmanager.com/